Shaping Long-Term Care in Emerging Asia

Countries are facing increasing life expectancy and a shrinking family size and in effect, this may escalate demands for medical and supportive services. The role of families in providing informal care will remain important. However, the simultaneous decline in the supply of informal caregiving caused by changes in family structure and higher female labour-market participation necessitates the expansion of the public role in care provision. This book analyses the challenges of long-term care (LTC) policy development and implications from advanced LTC systems and a current trajectory in emerging economies in Asia.

The book approaches the subject through comparative analysis on what works and what does not to provide insight into public policy options for sustainable LTC provision and financing mechanisms. How the countries adopt different approaches to health and social systems towards LTC development could provide important insight and perspectives into policy options in the region.

This book aims at academics, policymakers, and practitioners in health, social, and aged care services and could also be used as a teaching resource for undergraduate students in health and social sciences and postgraduate programs in public health, epidemiology, social demography, gerontology, and nursing. The book will be of interest to a wider audience not only on social and health consequences of population ageing but also on health and social policy relating to older persons.

Vasoontara S. Yiengprugsawan is a social epidemiologist and has over 15 years' experience in development and public health in academia and policy research with international organisations. She held senior research positions (University of New South Wales and Australian National University), a Fellowship with the World Health

Organization Asia Pacific Observatory on Health Systems and Policies, and an Australian Endeavour Fellowship.

John Piggott is Director of the Australian Research Council Centre of Excellence in Population Ageing Research (CEPAR) at the University of New South Wales, where he is Scientia Professor of Economics. He has published widely on issues in retirement and pension economics and finance in the leading international economics and actuarial academic journals.

Routledge Advances in Asia-Pacific Studies

For more information about this series, please visit: www.routledge.com/Routledge-Advances-in-Asia-Pacific-Studies/book-series/SE0453

Shaping Long-Term Care in Emerging Asia

Policy and Country Experiences

Edited by
**Vasoontara S. Yiengprugsawan
and John Piggott**

Routledge
Taylor & Francis Group

LONDON AND NEW YORK

First published 2023
by Routledge
4 Park Square, Milton Park, Abingdon, Oxon OX14 4RN

and by Routledge
605 Third Avenue, New York, NY 10158

Routledge is an imprint of the Taylor & Francis Group, an informa business

British Library Cataloguing-in-Publication Data
A catalogue record for this book is available from the British Library

Library of Congress Cataloging-in-Publication Data
Names: Yiengprugsawan, Vasoontara Sbirakos, editor. | Piggott,
John (John R.), editor.
Title: Shaping long-term care in emerging Asia : policy and country
experiences / edited by Vasoontara Sbirakos Yiengprugsawan and
John Piggott AO.
Description: Abingdon, Oxon ; New York, NY : Routledge, 2023. |
Series: Routledge advances in Asia-Pacific studies | Includes bibliographical
references and index. |
Identifiers: LCCN 2022042131 | ISBN 9780367674588 (hardback) |
ISBN 9780367674595 (paperback) | ISBN 9781003131373 (ebook)
Subjects: LCSH: Older people—Care—Government policy—Asia. |
Long term care of the sick—Government policy—Asia.
Classification: LCC HV1484.A782 S53 2023 | DDC 362.6095—dc23/eng/20221123
LC record available at https://lccn.loc.gov/2022042131

ISBN: 9780367674588 (hbk)
ISBN: 9780367674595 (pbk)
ISBN: 9781003131373 (ebk)

DOI: 10.4324/9781003131373

Typeset in Times New Roman
by codeMantra

To Myria Anantara for strength and inspiration.

Contents

Figures

Tables

Contributors

Lu Bei is at the ARC Centre of Excellence in Population Ageing Research, University of New South Wales, Australia.

Dai-Thu Bui is at the Institute of Social and Medical Studies, Ha Noi, Vietnam.

Nalinee N. Chuakhamfoo is at the Centre for Health Equity Monitoring Foundation, Phitsanulok, Thailand.

Thanh-Long Giang is at National Economics University, Hanoi, Vietnam.

Dinar Kharisma is at Kementerian Perencanaan Pembangunan Nasional (BAPPENAS)/Ministry of National Development Planning of the Republic of Indonesia.

Maliki is at Kementerian Perencanaan Pembangunan Nasional (BAPPENAS)/Ministry of National Development Planning of the Republic of Indonesia.

Supasit Pannarunothai is at the Centre for Health Equity Monitoring Foundation, Phitsanulok, Thailand.

John Piggott is at the Australian Research Council Centre of Excellence in Population Ageing Research (ARC CEPAR), University of New South Wales, Australia.

Rosinta H.P. Purba is at Kementerian Perencanaan Pembangunan Nasional (BAPPENAS)/Ministry of National Development Planning of the Republic of Indonesia.

Nurlina Supartini is at the Ministry of Health, Jakarta, Republic of Indonesia.

Thai-Quang Trinh is at the Vietnam Academy of Social Sciences, Ha Noi, Vietnam.

Vasoontara S. Yiengprugsawan is at the Australian Research Council Centre of Excellence in Population Ageing Research (ARC CEPAR), University of New South Wales, Australia.

Foreword

Driven by rapid demographic transition, over the past decade aged care systems in East and Southeast Asia have moved from the margins of policymaker attention to presenting some of the most interesting and complex social policy challenges. In a region where family based support remains the dominant mode of care for the overwhelming majority of older people, the sense of urgency in several countries around defining the appropriate and sustainable role of the state and the market as complements to families is striking. At the same time, the state of aged care system development across the region is also varied, reflecting underlying demographic and social forces, administrative and fiscal capacity, healthcare and social security systems, and other factors.

In this context, better understanding of cross-country commonalities and differences in aged care system development in emerging Asia has become vitally important, both within countries and to promote learning across them. This collection of country case studies from China, Thailand, Indonesia, and Vietnam is a valuable addition to the state of knowledge in the sector. It combines a synthesis of cross-country policy challenges and emerging lessons with deep dives on the distinctive features of each country's approach to building their aged care sector. The state of play across – and within – the four countries demonstrates that aged care in the region is a sector facing many common challenges but with diverse approaches to navigating them. As in richer countries, there is not a single model for aged care systems which will suit all situations.

The common challenges facing the countries covered in the collection, apart from societal ageing itself, include the sectoral policy and governance framework, how to finance formal aged care systems in sustainable, equitable and efficient ways, expanding coverage of care services and the human resources to provide them, and striking the appropriate balance between home- and community-based and residential care. Each of these challenges raises questions of the appropriate and sustainable roles of the state, the market, and households in the provision and financing of aged care, as well as how to build complementarity between informal sources of care and formal arrangements.

In addition to illustrating how each country is navigating these common challenges, the individual case studies go deeper on distinctive elements of the emerging approach in each country. In China, the focus is on aged care financing pilots through the social insurance system, with subnational variations which demonstrate a flexible approach which is likely to, in turn, inform future national policy developments. Thailand is leveraging its healthcare system, in particular its strong primary care network, and gradually structuring home- and community-based services as part of its wider commitment to universal health care. While Vietnam is at an earlier stage of building its aged care system, it is placing a strong emphasis on the role of communities and older people themselves in care support, through Intergenerational Self-Help Clubs and community-based volunteers. As the youngest country in the group, Indonesia is proactively piloting a range of approaches, mainly building on its primary care network, but also involving communities and innovating with information systems on older persons. Each of these experiences offers insights for other developing countries. They also show systems that are very much work in progress.

I hope that policymakers, practitioners, researchers, and other development players will enjoy and learn from the rich experiences highlighted in this collection. Building formal aged care systems and incorporating informal care will be an unavoidable challenge for many developing countries and the experience of the pioneers in this collection should be of great value.

Philip O'Keefe, Professor of Practice
Director, Ageing in Asia Research Hub
ARC Centre of Excellence in Population
Ageing Research (CEPAR)
University of New South Wales, Australia

Acknowledgement

This research was funded by the Australian Research Council Centre of Excellence in Population Ageing Research (ARC CEPAR), grant number CE1701005. This book is part of a larger initiative on ageing in Asia which had its origins in a Rockefeller Bellagio Residency awarded to John Piggott.

The editors and chapter authors would like to thank Peter Sbirakos and Anne Charlotte-Stent for their editorial guidance on earlier drafts.

1 Setting the scene

*Vasoontara S. Yiengprugsawan
and John Piggott*

In the sphere of social protection, long-term care (LTC), or aged care, has gained political and public interest over the past few decades. Throughout the developed world, almost without exception, populations are ageing and LTC policies are evolving (OECD, 2011). Ad hoc approaches to LTC support are giving way to systematic policy structures, providing frameworks within which households and families can prepare contingency plans for older members requiring LTC support. At the same time, policy imperatives are moving away from institutional care towards care in the home or the community. Major issues remain such that informal caregivers face an escalating tension between work and care; funding is often inadequate; processes to establish eligibility are slow and requirements for recipients or their families to meet out-of-pocket expenses are frequently complex. Nevertheless, LTC protection is gradually being established as an important social protection offered by the state, to complement retirement income and health services, for those whose needs have been established, and earning capacity exhausted.

In developing countries, by contrast, LTC policy is in its development phase. In many emerging economies in Asia, shrinking family size, increased female labour force participation, and greater regional/rural-urban migration have placed unprecedented pressures on the traditional role of family care provision for the elderly (WHO, 2015; World Bank, 2016). Many of these countries face these challenges with limited resources, a less developed formal workforce, and an underdeveloped welfare system where almost 65% of the workforce is employed in informal sectors (ILO, 2018).

Populations aged 60 years and over, within emerging economies of the East and Southeast regions of Asia, will increase from 320 million to 543 million within the next 15 years. By 2035, the percentage of people aged 60 and over will reach 16% in Indonesia, 28% in China, and 30.5% in Thailand (United Nations, 2019). Among older population

DOI: 10.4324/9781003131373-1

groups, chronic non-communicable diseases (NCDs) such as diabetes and heart conditions are the most common with the requirement for a comprehensive and continuation model of care (Global Burden of Diseases, 2019). Notably, with the global threat of the coronavirus (*COVID-19*), the risk for severe illness increases with age, with *older adults* at the highest risk (HelpAge, 2020; WHO, 2020).

Combined with declining fertility, rapid urbanisation, and rising inequality, it is inevitable that many millions of older people will confront severe hardship over the coming decades unless the issue of LTC support in emerging economies receives systematic attention and appropriate structures and services are developed (World Bank, 2016; ADB, 2022). LTC is provided in three broadly defined settings—home, community, and institutions—which include medical as well as social care services (e.g., assistance with daily activities and other social support structures). LTC systems are commonly linked to existing health system structures and health-social welfare boundaries. The significance of the provision and funding of LTC for older person concerns not only the socioeconomic well-being of older persons, their immediate families and communities, labour market implications of caregivers, but ultimately also impacts the sustainability of healthcare and social service systems at a national level. This book is in response to the critical need to advance knowledge and policy development on LTC in emerging economies that also fit well under the international United Nations 2030 Sustainable Development Goals and the World Health Organization's Decade of Healthy Ageing (2020–2030) in promoting functional ability and well-being in older age.

The book first introduces LTC typologies and the challenges of LTC policy development and implications from advanced LTC systems in Asia (Chapter 1). It then discusses social and economic contexts, including labour markets and overarching social security profiles, and health systems within the context of emerging economies (Chapter 2). The country case study chapters include current LTC policy and related programs from the selected emerging economies—China, Thailand, Vietnam, and Indonesia—and range from existing pilot projects to community-based LTC models (Chapters 3–6). Four main themes between health and LTC service provisions are linked, including public insurance and social welfare for older persons, public-private financing mechanisms for health and LTC services, current informal-formal care arrangements, and LTC workforce considerations. Lastly, Chapter 7 synthesises the four country case studies drawing on common challenges and potential LTC models within each country's health and social context. Critically examining the current provision and financing, as well as the trajectory of these programs may shed light on the feasibility of LTC and the support mechanisms required in emerging economies.

Conceptual framework: healthy ageing and long-term care

WHO's Decade of Healthy Ageing (2021–2030) focuses on "the process of developing and maintaining the functional ability that enables well-being in older age". It considers an individual's functional ability to be, and to do, the things they value. This functional ability is determined not just by an individual's intrinsic capacity (influenced by diseases), but also by the environment (e.g., home, community, or broader society) they inhabit and the care and support that is available to them (WHO, 2015). Subject to an older person's individual capacity, their trajectory interacts with and requires health and LTC services at different stages (Figure 1.1).

A decline in capacity is part of a continuum and in some older persons, the decline may be preventable, delayed onsets, or reversible. For example, for those in the high and stable capacity level, chronic NCDs may be mitigated by reducing health risk behaviours (e.g., smoking and drinking) and maintaining healthy lifestyles (through nutrition and physical activity). For those with declining or risk of significant loss of capacity, both medical health services and non-medical health

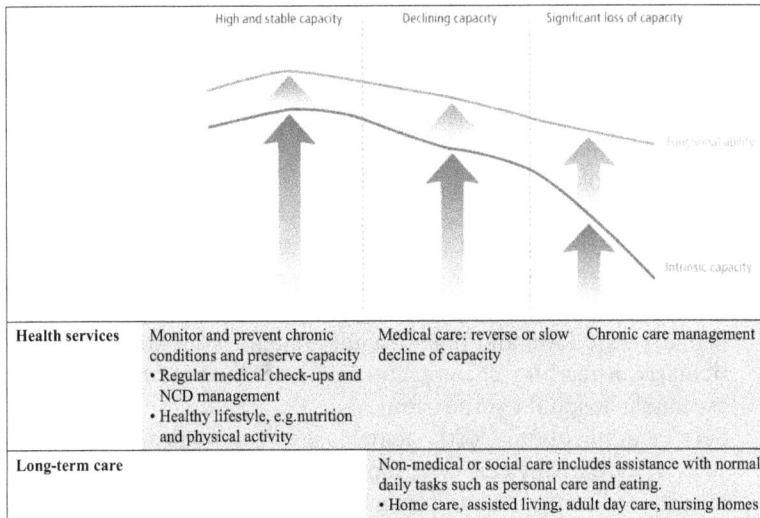

	High and stable capacity	Declining capacity	Significant loss of capacity
Health services	Monitor and prevent chronic conditions and preserve capacity • Regular medical check-ups and NCD management • Healthy lifestyle, e.g. nutrition and physical activity	Medical care: reverse or slow decline of capacity	Chronic care management
Long-term care		Non-medical or social care includes assistance with normal daily tasks such as personal care and eating. • Home care, assisted living, adult day care, nursing homes	

Figure 1.1 Capacity levels and services, WHO Healthy Ageing framework

4 *Vasoontara S. Yiengprugsawan and John Piggott*

services are required. These support mechanisms are crucial and can assist an older person to maintain a level of functional ability and dignity despite physical and cognitive decline.

Health and long-term care systems

Health and LTC systems are linked, often overlap, and encompass chronic and complex medical needs. Health services for older persons often involve all levels of health services from primary health care to tertiary, rehabilitation, and palliative care. LTC can include a range of services and multiple providers. There are often multiple settings, e.g. home, community, and institutions, and LTC involves both medical and non-medical personnel, e.g. caregivers, doctors, nurses and specialists, and community and social workers.

Health care is necessary but not sufficient for long-term care

The rise in NCDs with age means both the absolute and relative shares of people living with chronic and often multiple conditions will increase (WHO, 2015; World Bank, 2016). Comorbidities require comprehensive health services and chronic care management between various levels within the health system. Three main common issues and gaps in the current healthcare delivery for older persons are as follows:

- Hospital-centric care with high-cost treatment. With ageing populations and NCDs, preventive and primary care services are essential in early diagnosis, prevention, and monitoring. In many settings, health care is often sought too late resulting in high-cost treatment in acute care hospitals. Primary health care is not fully utilised for older persons and NCDs.
- Poorly coordinated care. Care is rarely coordinated across provider levels, resulting in a lack of continuity of health care and out-of-pocket expenditure despite universal health care. The lack of effective referrals and challenges with gatekeeping roles at the primary care level and post-discharge home from hospitals, particularly crucial for chronic conditions, contribute to costly but avoidable hospital readmissions.
- Service duplication. Costly acute care hospitals provide services such as outpatient care and inpatients acute care. The spike in hospital utilisation rates among older persons and the high average lengths of hospital stays in China suggest that hospitals have been inefficiently used as nursing homes for the elderly.

Definitions

LTC (health and social) is defined by the Organisation for Economic Co-operation and Development (OECD) as consisting of

> a range of medical, personal care and assistance services that are provided with the primary goal of alleviating pain and reducing or managing the deterioration in health status for people with a degree of long-term dependency, assisting them with their personal care through help for activities of daily living (ADLs), including both "body-touch" care such as for bathing and toileting, and through help for instrumental activities of daily living (IADL) or "non-body-touch" care such as for meal preparation, cleaning, shopping, and managing finance which help care recipients to live independently.

According to the US National Institute on Ageing,

> long-term care involves a variety of services designed to meet a person's health or personal care needs during a short or long period of time. These services help people live as independently and safely as possible when they can no longer perform everyday activities on their own.

The World Bank's definition has further distinguished health from LTC as follows: "…[LTC] is quite distinct from health care in that while healthcare services seek to change the health condition (from unwell to well), LTC services seek to make the current condition (frail or unwell) more bearable". In some contexts, LTC health components include palliative care and nursing care, while the social component includes home help and residential care services.

Typologies

LTC systems are generally funded through government taxes and/or by social security contributions. An earlier report by the OECD (2011) described three country categories based on the scope of LTC entitlement and coverage: (1) countries with universal coverage within a single program, e.g. through tax-based funding mechanisms such as in Denmark, Finland, and Sweden in Scandinavia, or through a social insurance such as in Germany, Japan, and the Republic of Korea, (2) a means-tested scheme such as in the USA and the UK, and (3) mixed systems such as in France and New Zealand.

A more recent typology of LTC financing mechanisms (WHO) has proposed to further separate single universal coverage and result in four types of LTC systems:

1. Single universal model which includes public LTC coverage separated from the health system such as in Scandinavia or through the health coverage in Belgium
2. Social insurance models which are financed through compulsory contributions such as through payroll taxes in Germany, Japan, and the Republic of Korea. These are often stand-alone (from health care), dedicated social insurance arrangements for LTC services
3. Means-tested systems, e.g. tax-based coverage dependent on eligibility thresholds in the USA
4. Parallel, hybrid, or mixed systems such as in France and Australia.

Each system has advantages and disadvantages in the areas of financing, eligibility, and overall benefits. While single-program universal arrangements have a wide coverage of LTC services, they generally occupy a larger share of a country's national income. Some other LTC systems may apply primarily to the older population or to all ages with care needs. Co-payments are generally required for personal care, subject to income thresholds, and social insurance. The mixed system relies on different coexisting coverage schemes; for example, skilled nursing-related care is provided through the health system while personal and social care is provided through a separate program. LTC financing mechanisms influence service delivery and its personnel. Some systems that do not cover personal care still leave these care responsibilities to family members.

LTC can be provided informally at home or formally through communities and institutions or residential programs. Home care is mostly provided through informal channel by family members, friends, volunteers, and in advanced economies through public home-based care and paid professionals. Broad trend in OECD countries in recent times has been towards increased use of home and community-based care where possible. LTC systems not only create more employment opportunities within communities but also relieve the care burden on family members.

Community services are support services that can, for example, include adult day care, meal programs, and senior centres. These can help people who are cared for at home, and their families. Residential facilities offer formal LTC services typically for older people who can no *longer* live at home. These could be in the form of independent living with on-site assistance for everyday personal care or institutional care with a comprehensive range of healthcare services.

One of the main concerns of LTC is quality assurance. Care provision by allied health professionals or formal caregivers is regulated to ensure minimum standards. The quality of LTC is assessed in three broad categories: effectiveness and safety, patient centeredness and responsiveness, and care coordination. Only some countries have implemented training for homecare and regular monitoring and reporting for public and private facilities.

Long-term care in East Asia: case studies of Japan and South Korea

As countries with the greatest ageing population in Asia, Japan, and South Korea are at the forefront of the LTC policy movement and can provide useful lessons from a regional context. Japan and South Korea both share strong traditional family values and cultural preferences for social care at home or in the community. Other common factors across the two countries include primary health and service provider networks that provide integral foundations for LTC development.

The choice of financing sources and systems in each country varies. Middle-income countries face difficult economic and political choices among the different financing sources for LTC benefits, especially between general tax-based systems and social insurance. Both Japan and South Korea have implemented a public LTC insurance (LTCI). The policy choice between universal or targeted LTC systems is also an issue for most governments in Asia, who are still working towards universal health coverage rather than universal access to LTC.

Using an LTC social insurance as a mechanism for financing LTC (adopted in Japan and South Korea) may provide a few lessons for emerging countries in Asia. *First,* the countries are familiar with the system since it is commonly used to finance medical care. *Second,* both countries started with less generous benefit packages and have expanded the benefits as more financing options have become available. There is a trade-off between population coverage, service packages, and fiscal sustainability. *Third,* both countries also use some forms of cost-sharing; for example, out-of-pocket payments are often utilised to discourage service overuse, in combination with subsidies for poor populations to maintain appropriate access. *Lastly,* Japan and South Korea are also moving towards community-based

LTC which is relevant to emerging economies in Asia having potential knowledge transferability on lessons learnt and pathways.

Development of long-term care policy

In contrast with countries in Europe (e.g., Germany) where the LTC system was developed for people with disabilities, including older people, LTC in Japan and South Korea was introduced in the context of population ageing (Rhee, Done & Anderson, 2015). People aged 65 years or older are eligible for all types of LTC, but eligibility for those under 65 is restricted to age-related LTC needs, such as individuals with geriatric diseases e.g., dementia and cerebrovascular disease. Although individuals between ages 40 and 64 pay into the system, they are limited in their access to benefits in both Japan and South Korea. The design of LTC, such that younger people contribute but their eligibility for benefits is restricted, has resulted in a large intergenerational transfer and has contributed to the financial sustainability of LTC.

When the LTC insurance system was originally established, it was separate from the medical insurance systems in both countries. For example, the Japanese LTC insurance system, through a decade-long process, began in 2000 with the "Ten Year Strategy to Promote Health and Welfare for the Elderly", informally known as the "Gold Plan". It introduced an insurance-based system, it was a user-oriented choice, and it was decentralised.

Inspired by the Japanese LTCI model, South Korea's law regarding LTCI for older adults was passed in the National Assembly's plenary session in 2007, and the program was implemented in July 2008. The rapid adoption of the LTCI was entrenched in the country's political-economic context overseen by the Ministry of Health and Welfare and operated by a single public insurer, the National Health Insurance Service (NHIS). Public care services for older persons who have difficulty performing daily living activities existed before 2008, and it was managed by local governments. However, the services were limited to impoverished older persons who had no family support, and most services were in the form of institutional care rather than home-based care.

Financing mechanisms for long-term care and eligibility

Under Japan's scheme, funding for the LTCI program is composed of tax revenues (50%) and premiums and co-payments from individuals aged 40 and above. Tax revenues are derived from both central and local taxes (25% national, 12.5% prefectures, and 12.5%

municipalities) In Japan's LTCI system, older adults who are certified for the LTCI service pay a 10% co-payment for services; the remaining 90% is covered by the LTCI budget (Ikegami, 2019; Yamada & Arai, 2020). Although it operates as a social insurance system, municipalities act as the insurers for LTCI and are responsible for setting budgets as well as premium levels for beneficiaries, including 47 prefectures and 3,300 municipalities.

Funding of South Korea's LTCI is separate from the NHIS (Jeon & Kwon, 2017; Kim & Kwon, 2021). The contribution rate is 6.55% of health insurance premiums; in other words, anyone who makes health insurance contributions also makes an LTCI contribution. The financing mix is composed of contributions (60%–65%), tax subsidies (20%), and co-payment by service users, which is 20% for institutional services and 15% for home-based services. The co-insurance rate for institutional care is higher than that for home-based care in order to promote home and community-based care (85%–100% for in-home services are covered). Overall, LTCI covers 80%–100% based on the beneficiaries' economic status and there is a substantial subsidy for co-payments for low-income groups.

In both countries, older adults aged 65 years or older or citizens younger than 65 years but with chronic illnesses or disabilities are eligible for LTCI. Among these, people who have difficulties in activities of daily living for at least six months are eligible for LTCI. LTCI benefits include both in-kind and cash benefits. In-kind benefits include home care and institutional care services. In Japan, the eligibility is determined by the two-step assessment process with a 74-item standardised questionnaire. To be admitted to nursing homes, the recipients should be levels 1 or 2; however, with the approval of the LTCI committee,

Textbox 1 Eligibility criteria for long-term care services

	Japan	*South Korea*
Eligibility criteria for LTC	The 74 items are classified into seven levels of activities of daily living requirements. Support levels 1 and 2 and care need levels 1 (least disabled) to 5 (most disabled).	Applicants who do not attain a score of >45 points are disqualified for LTCI Level 1: need help in all aspects (>95) L2: need help in most aspects (75 to ≤95) L3 need help in some parts (60 to <75) L4: need help for daily living because of functional disability (50 to <60) L5: dementia patients (45 to <50)

people who are in levels 3–5 can also be admitted. In South Korea, a 90-item LTCI checklist is categorised into 11 sections, including ADL, cognition level, behavioural changes, need for nursing care, need for rehabilitation, need for welfare medical devices, state of care, environmental evaluation, visual/hearing ability, and diseases or symptoms.

In Japan, LTCI services are provided to insured persons who are certified for support or care requirements according to their care needs and certification assessment (Yamada & Ara, 2020). Dependent older adults can select and use provided facilities such as in-home or community-based services. The insurance benefits include in-home services (e.g., home visits/day services and short-stay services/care) and services at facilities, including LTC welfare facilities (also called special nursing homes), LTC health facilities (also called geriatric health services facilities), and LTC medical facilities (medical LTC sanatoriums).

In South Korea, LTC hospitals (LTCHs) provide another distinct form of LTC. They deliver various medical services, including subacute services to LTC, palliative care, and rehabilitation services. As of 2020, there were 1,481 LTCHs in South Korea (Ga, 2020). One of the challenges associated with the lack of coordination between health care and LTC includes overlapping services provided by LTC institutions (which are covered by LTCI) and LTCHs (which are covered by NHI). As the benefits package under NHI tends to be more generous than that under LTCI, there is a financial incentive for longer lengths of stay in LTCHs.

Textbox 2 Available long-term care services

	Japan	South Korea
LTC services	Support levels 1 and 2: Care plan for preventive long-term care services such as outpatient rehabilitation, home-visit services, and community-based services. Care levels 1–5: Facility services such as intensive care homes and sanatorium medical facilities. In-home services including home-visit nursing during the day and at night, and short-stay admission services.	The seven types of home care services: (1) day/night care centre services, (2) home-visit care services by LTC assistants, (3) home-visit services to promote cognition activities, (4) home-visit nursing services by nurses, dental hygienists, or nursing assistants, (5) home-visit bathing services, (6) short-term institutionalised care, and (7) provision of welfare devices.

The LTCI scheme has not only created more employment opportunities but it has also relieved the care burden on families. Each LTC facility generally includes a medical doctor, nurses, nursing assistants, a physiotherapist, and social workers. There is also an increasing number of family members completing formal training courses offered by the Government to become qualified as formal caregivers and case managers. There is a national certification system for LTC workers to ensure quality of care. The certification course comprises two parts: 240 hours of training (theory, practice, and apprenticeship) and the qualification examination. All LTCI service providers are required to hire only certified elderly care workers. Home-based care and institutional care service providers are evaluated biannually. The quality of nursing homes is assessed every three years and announced publicly.

Integrated community care systems

An "integrated community care" model has been introduced to the LTC to assist older persons so they can remain living in their homes as long as possible rather than entering residential aged care. In Japan, the integrated community care system was introduced by an amendment to the Long-Term Care Insurance Act and implemented in April 2012. Community-based LTC services are provided by a mix of private, public, and non-profit organisations. Both the Japanese central government and local municipality governments have been promoting community group activities resulting in a more diverse service system, tailored to the circumstances of each area. Through this system, aged care is centred at home and services are coordinated by the Integrated Community Care Centre (Morikawa, 2014). To receive appropriate care, older persons move between different types of care facilities.

While nursing homes and LTCHs are currently a common solution for older adults requiring LTC in South Korea, the Ministry of Health and Welfare launched a social service policy in 2018 for community care projects, which provide integrated support for lodging, health care, day care, and independent livelihood to people in their own homes. The current trial implementation runs until 2022 and a full roll-out will occur after 2025.

Concluding notes

Community LTC supplementing home care services as adopted in Japan and South Korea aligns with existing networks which could be economically achievable and sustainable in emerging Asian economies. The integrated system would require effective coordination and transition across a continuum of care for older persons from preventive health and hospital services to home care and community-based facilities. In laying the foundations for LTC systems and ensuring sustainability of LTC services, low- and middle-income countries will need to take into account existing health systems and social service structures, their coverage, accessibility, and financing.

References

ADB. 2022. *The Road to Better Long-Term Care in Asia and the Pacific: Building Systems of Care and Support for Older Persons.* Asian Development Bank, Manila.

Ga H. 2020. Long-term care system in Korea. *Annals of Geriatric Medicine and Research.* 24(3): 181–186.

Global Burden of Disease. 2019. *GBD Data Visualization. Institute for Health Metrics and Evaluation.* University of Washington, Seattle.

HelpAge International. 2020. COVID-19 and Older People in Asia Pacific 2020 in review. United Nations Population Funds, HelpAge International Asia Pacific Regional Office, Chiang Mai.

Ikegami N. 2019. Financing long-term care: Lessons from Japan. *International Journal of Health Policy and Management.* 8(8): 462–466.

International Labour Office. 2018. *Women and Men in the Informal Economy: A Statistic Picture.* ILO, Geneva.

Jeon B & Kwon S. 2017. Health and long-term care systems for older people in the Republic of Korea: Policy challenges and lessons. *Health Systems & Reform.* 3(3): 214–233.

Kim H & Kwon S. 2021. A decade of public long-term care insurance in South Korea: Policy lessons for aging countries. *Health Policy.* 125(1): 22–26.

Laguna EP. 2020. Caregiving in Vietnamese Families. In Vu NC. et al. (Eds). *Ageing and Health in Viet Nam.* Economic Research Institute for ASEAN and East Asia (ERIA), Jakarta.

Morikawa M. 2014. Towards community-based integrated care: trends and issues in Japan's long-term care policy. *International Journal of Integrated Care.* doi: 10.5334/ijic.1066/.

OECD. 2011. *Help Wanted? Providing and Paying for Long-Term Care.* Organisation for Economic Co-operation and Development, Paris.

Rhee JC, Done N, & Anderson G. 2015. Considering long-term care insurance for middle-income countries: comparing South Korea with Japan and Germany. *Health Policy.* 119(10): 1319–1329.

Royal Commission into Aged Care Quality and Safety. 2020. *Review of International Systems for Long-Term Care of Older People.* Commonwealth of Australia, Canberra.

Tsuita Y, Komazawa O. 2020. *Human Resources for the Health and Long-Term Care of Older Persons in Asia.* Economic Research Institute for ASEAN and East Asia (ERIA), Jakarta and Institute of Developing Economies, Japan External Trade Organization, (IDE–JETRO) Tokyo.

United Nations. 2019. *World Population Prospects.* Department of Economic and Social Affairs. UN Population Division: New York.

WHO. 2015. *World Report on Ageing and Health.* World Health Organization.

WHO. 2017. *Integrated Care for Older People: Guidelines on Community-Level Interventions to Manage Declines in Intrinsic Capacity.* World Health Organization, Geneva.

WHO. 2020. *Coronavirus disease (COVID-19): Risks and safety for older people.* World Health Organization, Geneva.

World Bank. 2016. *Live Long and Prosper: Aging in East Asia and Pacific.* World Bank, Washington DC.

World Bank. 2017. *Aging and Long-Term Care Systems: A Review of Finance and Governance Arrangements in Europe, North America and Asia-Pacific.* World Bank, Washington, DC.

Yamada M & Arai H. 2022. Long-term care system in Japan. *Annals of Geriatric Medicine and Research.* 24(3): 174–180.

2 Ageing, health, and social transitions in selected emerging Asian economies

Vasoontara S. Yiengprugsawan and John Piggott

Demographic drivers

According to the United Nations Population Division estimates (United Nations, 2019), countries in East and Southeast Asia are ageing more rapidly than any other regions around the world. In 2020, countries in the region had almost 400 million people aged 60 years and older, with roughly 37% (almost 250 million) of the global population of this age group within the Chinese mainland alone. In contrast, Japan completed its transition to an ageing society decades ago whilst South Korea will catch up in the next three decades. By 2050, close to 45% of the population of Japan and South Korea will be aged 60 years and above. Currently, the population aged 60 years and older in China and Thailand represent 17% and 19%, respectively, and both proportions are projected to increase to almost 30% in the next 15 years. In Vietnam and Indonesia, the older population represents 10% and 12%, respectively, with a projected upward trajectory in the coming decades (United Nations, 2019).

Another major demographic change is driven by a rapid decline in fertility (United Nations, 2019). Rates declined dramatically from 2.83 children per woman in 1980 to 1.81 in 2020 in the East and Southeast Asian regions—significantly faster than the global estimate of 3.59 and 2.42, respectively. Historically, fertility rates in East Asian countries, particularly in Japan and South Korea, remain among the lowest in the world (1.3 and 1.9, respectively). In China and Thailand, the fertility rates are well below replacement fertility and continue to fall. Vietnam and Indonesia share similar trajectories of fertility rates with over 5 in 1980, followed by a substantial decline to 2 and 2.5 in 2000, and 2 and 2.3 in 2020, respectively (United Nations, 2019).

As a result of population ageing and low fertility rates, the total dependency ratio (ratio of population aged 0–24 and 65+ per 100

DOI: 10.4324/9781003131373-2

population 25–64 years old) and potential support ratio (per population aged 65 years and older) have shifted towards putting greater pressure on the working-age population. These have implications for labour force pensions, health care, and social welfare.

Epidemiologic drivers

Along with demographic changes, East and Southeast Asia are also experiencing rapid epidemiological transitions. As people live longer, causes of morbidity and mortality have shifted towards chronic non-communicable diseases (NCDs). Cardiovascular disease, cancers, and diabetes account for the bulk of all disability-adjusted life years (DALYs) among those aged 60 years and over with comorbidities complicating treatments and requiring continuity of care. NCDs cause the majority of deaths in the region, notably 74%, 76%, 79%, and 88% in Thailand, Indonesia, Vietnam, and China in 2019, respectively (Global Burden of Disease, 2019). Premature death and disability were associated with NCD-related risk factors such as tobacco use and alcohol abuse, high salt intake, high cholesterol, high blood sugar, and physical inactivity globally. These lifestyle-related conditions accumulated throughout the life course have now resulted in the onset of hypertension and obesity from earlier life (Asia Pacific Observatory on Health Systems and Policies, 2016).

COVID-19 and older persons

In late 2019, the COVID-19 pandemic emerged worldwide with older adults not only disproportionately affected but also experiencing greater vulnerabilities and complications post-recovery (ADB 2021; WHO 2020). The COVID-19 pandemic has increased caregiving responsibilities in families and disrupted the delivery of community-based and residential care. The pandemic presents a unique opportunity for many countries to strengthen their health and LTC systems, including community-based services and the upskilling of volunteer networks to enable older adults to continue living in their home environment.

Health system responsiveness

Health systems in emerging Asian economies are still preparing for population ageing and NCDs. Despite the increase in overall health expenditure (and specifically government expenditure on health), out-of-pocket expenditure (OOP) has generally declined as the countries are moving towards Universal Health Coverage (UHC). Notably, the significant decrease in OOP in Thailand from 34% to 11% is directly attributed to the successful implementation of the country's nationwide UHC. Health infrastructure and the number of healthcare professionals also vary substantially across the country case studies with differing availabilities and levels of investments in their respective health systems.

According to the World Health Organization's Global Health Observatory, the ratios of hospital beds per 1,000 population range from 1.2 in Indonesia, to twice that number in Thailand and Vietnam, and over four times in China. The proportion of doctors were significantly higher in China (17.8 per 10,000 population) compared to about 8 in Thailand and Vietnam, and 3.8 in Indonesia. However, the density of nurses and midwives was highest in Thailand, 30.0 per 10,000 population, compared to about 20 in China and Indonesia, which is partly attributed to the role of primary health care.

These four countries are also at different stages of their health systems coverage. Thailand and China have moved further along in their implementation of UHC in the past two decades, whilst Vietnam and Indonesia have made rapid progress in expanding health systems coverage in the past decade. Notably, the emphasis has almost entirely been on expanding coverage through general revenue financing for those with the lowest income group. However, one common issue in emerging economies is that health insurance is often fragmented, with separate schemes for the civil service, state-owned enterprises, and private sector, which often leads to variable benefits. These differences could exacerbate inequalities such as the distinct rural and urban systems in China.

Socioeconomic drivers

A number of key social and economic factors play an important role in government policies in social protection, health, and LTC. Inequality is observed across and within countries, also exhibiting, gender disparities, and inter-generational differences. The four middle-income country case studies are at different economic development levels and varying degrees of relative inequalities. All countries have increased their Gross National Income (GNI) per capita and share of urban population over the past two decades. Despite economic growth, unequal urban and rural development has been a key push factor and a key driver of internal migration in the region. Notably, China has the lowest poverty headcount but the highest income inequality. Vietnam has the highest poverty headcount with a relatively low urban population although they have seen a steady rise in urban population growth from 24% in 2000 to 37% in 2019 (World Bank Open Data).

Informal sector and labour force participation

Emerging economies often have a large informal workforce, approximately 1.3 billion people in Asia according to the International Labour Office estimates, and there are also notable variations in labour force participation by gender and urban-rural areas (ILO, 2018). Homemakers are often females and agriculture and its related activities in rural areas are often classified as informal and unpaid. While female labour force participation has generally increased over time in the region, it is still generally less than half of the total labour force, and the lowest reported in Indonesia. Rural residents are almost twice as likely to be in informal work as those in urban areas, with the proportion in the agriculture sector estimated at more than 70% (ILO, 2018).

Informality means a lack of social protection, rights at work, and decent working conditions. In particular, female homemakers and rural informal workers are at a greater disadvantage than workers in urban areas as they are not entitled to social and retirement benefits, which could have adverse impacts as they age. The withdrawal of urban women from formal work for family reasons also limits these women's access to a formal sector pension and inadequacy due to lower contribution density.

Social protection system

There are variations in social protection across rural and urban areas in emerging Asia. Older persons continue to rely heavily on their own labour and the support of their families, in rural areas, while in urban formal workers, pensions play an important role. These economies are grappling with challenges of improving the sustainability of their existing pension systems and trying to expand these to the informal sector. However, the expansion of formal contributory schemes has been slow, and informal workers are overwhelmingly not covered by such schemes. With the exception of Indonesia, social pensions have been a common response to low coverage of formal schemes (Kudrna, O'Keefe, Piggott, 2021).

The expansion of coverage of informal rural and urban workers in China since 2010 through public subsidies represents the single biggest increase in contributors to a government pension system, though adequacy remains a major issue for informal workers. This incentive is important because contributions for these informal sector workers are voluntary. However, within China, differences between rural and urban areas are sharp. In Thailand, the expansion of social pensions has been more gradual, taking place over roughly a five-year period until a modest social pension could be achieved universally among the elderly that did not qualify for a formal pension. In Vietnam, coverage of formal schemes is around one quarter of workers, while social pensions are universal for those aged 80 and over, but are means tested for those aged 60–79. However, social pensions pay very low benefits. In Indonesia, where informality is high and pension and social assistance systems are underdeveloped, there is a large gap in terms of income protection for the elderly, with no significant social pension and formal schemes covering only around one in ten workers. Despite the broad social pension coverage that has now emerged in most of these countries, the level of social pensions in both absolute and relative terms is too low to provide adequate financial protection at older ages.

Co-residency and informal care

Co-residence of older people with adult children is high in East and Southeast Asia, although it varies across countries and has declined significantly over time in some. Co-residence with children has been declining rapidly, especially in urban China and Thailand. The main reasons come from demographic drivers (falling fertility resulting in small family sizes) as well as socioeconomic drivers (urban migration for job opportunities). However, across the four countries, multigenerational households are still relatively common in rural areas with cultural norms of family care for older persons, especially amongst daughters and daughters-in-law (World Bank, 2016). Social expectations of the roles of families, communities, and government are changing rapidly. Due to an increase in female labour force participation and smaller households, it has become increasingly difficult to leave the caregiving responsibility to the family. It has become an imperative for national governments to organise care services for older persons.

Reliance on informal family caregivers for older persons poses a number of social and economic challenges (Kristani et al., 2018, Wang et al., 2021, Yiengprugsawan et al., 2016). Family caregivers are untrained and have limited knowledge about the medical conditions of care recipients such as stroke, cancer, and dementia, which could have adverse impacts on the quality of care. Caregivers who have insufficient support (financial and/or non-financial) and who often face burnout, especially with the lack of respite care options. Spouses who are caregivers are especially at risk as they themselves may often require care due to poor physical or psychological health. Family caregivers are regarded as a shadow workforce with opportunity costs (such as not being in labour workforce) not formally accounted for. These family caregivers, who are mostly commonly female, are disadvantaged financially with respect to both direct out-of-pocket expenses and retirement security.

Encouraging formal care to complement informal care would allow women to increase their labour force participation. However, female family members that exit the labour force (or reduce their hours) forego income, benefits, and career opportunities in order to provide care and often have difficulty returning to work with less job flexibility in the workplace. Allowances for caregivers, where they are available, are too limited for economic independence to support themselves and their older care recipients. LTC systems can boost economic growth by freeing up informal caregivers for labour market participation while maintaining social cohesion.

Concluding notes

A range of demographic, epidemiological, and socioeconomic factors are driving an increased demand beyond informal care. An effective LTC system will also ensure that family caregivers are adequately trained and there is access to services such as respite care to reduce the burden on caregivers. Planning for LTC systems should also be taken into account and the older person's and their family's values and preferences.

References

ADB. 2021. Pandemic Preparedness and Response Strategies. Manila: Asian Development Bank. Retrieved from adb.org/publications/pandemic-preparedness-covid-19-lessons

Asia Pacific Observatory on Health Systems and Policies. 2016. Health system responses to population ageing and noncommunicable diseases in Asia. In Yiengprugsawan V, Healy J, Kendig H (Eds.). Vol. 2. No. 2. *World Health Organization*. Regional Office for Southeast Asia, New Delhi.

Global Burden of Disease. 2019. *GBD Data Visualization. Institute for Health Metrics and Evaluation*. University of Washington, Seattle.

International Labour Office. 2018. *Women and Men in the Informal Economy: A Statistic Picture*. ILO, Geneva.

Kristani MS, Engels Y, Effendy C, Astuti, Utarini A, Vernooij-Dassen M. 2018. Comparison of the lived experiences of family caregivers of patients with dementia and of patients with cancer in Indonesia. *International Psychogeriatrics*. 30(6): 903–914.

Kudrna G, O'Keefe P, Piggott J. 2021. Pension Policy in Emerging Asian Economies with Population Ageing: What Do We Know, Where Should We go? *CEPAR Working Paper 2021/2013*.

United Nations. 2019. *World Population Prospects. Department of Economic and Social Affairs*. UN Population Division, New York.

Wang Y, Ding L, Feng Y, Tang X, Sun L, Zhou C 2021. The effect of socio-economic status on informal caregiving for patents among adult married females: evidence from China. *BMC Geriatrics*. 21 (164): 1–9. doi:10.1186/s12877-021-02094-0

World Bank. 2016. *Live Long and Prosper: Aging in East Asia and Pacific*. World Bank, Washington, DC.

Yiengprugsawan V, Leach LS, Berecki-Gisolf J, Kendig H, Harley D, Seubsman S, Sleigh AC. 2016. Caregiving and mental health among workers: longitudinal evidence from a large cohort of adults in Thailand. *Social Science and Medicine – Population Health*. 2: 149–154.

3 China long-term care programs

Lu Bei

Introduction

Although China is one of the most rapidly ageing countries in the world, the amounting demand for public long-term care (LTC) still has a short window of opportunity, with the number of old people above the age of 80 just starting to surge (Lu et al. 2019, p. 120). Bloom et al. (2015) predict that an unprecedented ageing population in China is expected around 2030. This ageing process is accompanied by a decline in informal support due to low fertility rates since the 1980s. LTC will soon be an imperative challenge at the top of China's social agenda.

Currently, the Chinese LTC system resembles a multi-output power strip, with several government agencies involved in various aspects of services for different groups of people in need. At least Ministry of Civil Affairs (MCA), Ministry of Human Resources and Social Security (MOHRSS), China Disabled Person's Federation, and the new National Healthcare Security Administration (NHSA) have been involved in the services for people with LTC needs. The most recent development is a social insurance policy for LTC needs, which was initiated by local governments about a decade ago. So far, the central government has officially announced 29 cities as participating in the pilot LTC social insurance project. In most cases, the long-term care insurance (LTCI) is financed by the current healthcare system.

In terms of the institutional settings for the LTC policy, there have been frequent changes over the past decade. Traditionally, LTC policy in China has mainly been handled by the MCA, with benefits also subsidized by the China Disabled Persons' Federation (CDPF). In preparation for a rapidly ageing population and its associated increase in demand for services, the MOHRSS begun to play an increasingly important role about a decade ago. At present, the LTCI

DOI: 10.4324/9781003131373-3

is administered by the newly established agency NHSA. The following section aims to provide a trajectory of the development of LTC services in China through its policy evolution.

Traditional long-term care policy

MCA's LTC policy has been strictly means tested and resource tested (including family support resources). Eligible "Five Protection Household (Wubaohu)" recipients are entitled support covering five basic needs: food, clothing, housing, medicine, and access to funeral services. These services are available if a person answers no to three questions— no ability to work, no other income source, and no family support. Though most beneficiaries are rural based and have multiple impairments, the subsidy per capita is limited. According to the MCA Office Document No 139, dated August 2020 (hereinafter MCA 139), in the first quarter of 2019, the total number of beneficiaries of these "Wubaohu" were about 4.7 million, including 4.4 million in rural areas, and the majority were elderly. For rural recipients, the average expenditure was RMB 7,880 (US$1,212) per person, while urban recipients received an average of RMB 12,542 (US$1,930) (exchange rate is USD: RMB = 1:6.5 and hereafter) per person (MCA 139, p. 11). MCA also subsidized 13.7 million disabled people, which also included the elderly.

Apart from "Wubaohu", MCA also manages the so called "Social Welfare Institutions" (Fu Li Yuan) which provide residential care services that are heavily subsidized by the government for eligible recipients; however, the waiting list is generally exceptionally long in major cities. In the early 2000s, MCA's work planning documents had a target number of LTC residential beds per thousand elders aged 60 and above. By the end of 2019, more than 8 million LTC beds were available, according to MCA, which equals about 35 beds per thousand above the age of 60. However, public residential care facilities (Fu LI Yuan) managed directly by MCA only had 376,000 beds (MCA139, p. 8). The remaining more than 7.6 million beds are public housing beds for the "Wubaohu" recipients as well as registered facilities provided by communities or the private sector (Office of MCA 2020, p. 11). A large proportion of these beds are not providing meaningful social or medical care to disabled elders with adequate public or social funding. The policy goal for the number of beds per 1,000 elders was abolished in 2021; instead, the target is to provide 55% of nursing beds for all LTC facilities (Ministry of MCA and NDRC 2021).

Another benefit related to LTC funding is MCA's "senior subsidy". Anyone aged above 80 would be eligible for additional subsidies, with additional amounts offered at ages 90 and 100. The subsidy is managed regionally, and the amounts sometimes vary at a district level within a city.

Development of long-term care insurance policy initiatives

In the anticipation of a boom in LTC demand due to an ageing population and reduced family support, key government bodies have issued multiple policy documents on LTC. In September 2011, the 12th Five-Year Development Plan of Undertaking on Ageing (2011–2015) was released. In December 2011, the Development Plan of the Elderly Service System (2011–2015) was released by the State Council. In 2012, the Law on Protection of the Rights and Interests of the Elderly (Amended) was passed by the National People's Congress (NPC). In 2013, Some Opinions on Accelerating the Development of Social Services for the Elderly was released by the State Council which was followed by the Guidance on Combining Medical Services with Elderly Care Service in 2015 (Glinskaya and Feng, 2018).

These policy guidelines greatly encouraged local governments to initiate their own LTC policies. For example, Qingdao experimented in extending hospital services to home and communities as early as 2006 for some patients who needed LTC. In 2012, Qingdao city implemented an LTCI policy for their urban residents who had employee medical care insurance, mainly for their long-term medical needs. Several reforms followed the initial guidelines, and eventually in 2016, the Qingdao LTCI program included rural residents and social care services. This represents quite a typical policy procedure in China under the terminology of "touching the stone when passing the river" by local and central governments. Local initiatives vary from one place to another as they are integrated into different healthcare systems managed by local health agencies. As a new insurance, benefit design, funding mechanisms, service delivery, provider qualifications, recipients' eligibility, as well as assessment criteria are all critical to the operation of such a program. Pilots by local governments have provided different models and valuable insights into the formation of the programs.

These pilot projects undergo several trials and experiments to perfect their efficiency and efficacy. They are then developed into national policies with justifications if approved by the central government. Several LTC pilots on regional levels, like Qingdao, were available in the early 2010s. In June 2016, the MOHRSS issued "Guidelines for Establishing Long-term Care Insurance System Pilots by MOHRSS" (MOHRSS, Document 2016–80). This document officially acknowledged the legitimacy of 15 regional LTCI pilots and indicated there would be a nationwide LTC national insurance in the future.

Since the 1990s, most social assistance has been managed by MCA while social insurance has been managed by MOHRSS in China. As explained, LTC has traditionally been part of social assistance under MCA. However, MOHRSS's document 2016–80 induced competition to LTC's institutional settings, which resulted in the MCA immediately issuing the MCA-2016–200 document in July 2016 together with the Ministry of Finance (MOF) stating: "Notice to support pilot programs of home care and communities LTC service reforms through central funding" (MCA 2016). The MCA-2016–200 called for regional governments to apply for funding to conduct pilot projects to initiate home and community care models. At the same time, MCA promoted vocational education for caregivers and explored LTC providers' services standardization and beneficiaries' assessment standards.

In early 2018, the NHSA was established. NHSA ends the fragmented management of China's medical insurance payment and medicine pricing system and runs directly under the State Council. NHSA took over all health-related insurance policies from MOHRSS. Its mission was to integrate the relevant responsibilities from MOHRSS, the Health and Family Planning Commission (HFPC), the Development and Reform Commission (DRC), and MCA including: (1) basic medical and maternity insurance responsibilities for urban employees and urban residents (MOHRSS), (2) the new rural cooperative medical responsibilities (HFPC), (3) the National Drug Commission's responsibilities for drug and medical service price management, and (4) MCA's responsibilities for medical assistance. NHSA also took over the administration power of the LTCI which ended the long-standing conflict between MCA and MOHRSS over its managing responsibilities. The first Director of NHSA is from the MOF, with three deputy Directors from DRC, MOHRSS, and HFPC, respectively.

In September 2020, NHSA issued Document (2020) No. 37 "Guiding Perspectives of the MOF of the National Healthcare Security Administration on Expanding the Pilot Program of the Long-term Care Insurance System". The newly added pilot regions extended to every province apart from the 15 original pilots implemented by MOHRSS in 2016 (MCA and MOF 2016). This document also confirms the start of NHSA's administration of the LTCI. It states that the LTCI would initially begin with members of the urban employee basic medical insurance (UEBMI) program. This would then be expanded to all residents at the discretion of regional selection practices, signalling the continuation of the regional pilot programs, for at least the foreseeable future.

Integration with the healthcare system

China's healthcare system has undergone several reforms in the past 30 years and the literature is abundant with analyses of its reforms (Blumenthal and Hsiao 2005 and 2015, Hu et al. 2019). Before the early 1980s, health care was almost free in China, but the quality of care varied dramatically from place to place, especially between rural and urban areas. The 1984 reform changed the funding of public hospitals and institutions, and health service providers have since then operated like for-profit organizations. As of 1999, 49% of urban Chinese employees were members of the Urban Employee Health Insurance Scheme (hereinafter referred to as UEIMS), mostly through government and state enterprises. UEIMS is administered by MOHRSS. As for rural areas, only 7% of the 900 million rural Chinese had any coverage (Blumenthal and Hsiao 2015). In 2003, the government launched its new cooperative healthcare insurance, called the Rural and Urban Residents Medical Insurance Scheme (RUMIS), thus greatly expanding the coverage of its healthcare insurance. RUMIS was under the management of the former Ministry of Health till 2020. In 2020, the government claimed that more than 95% of the nation's individuals are covered by health insurance (NHSA 2021).

China's healthcare system is decentralized at a local jurisdiction level, mostly within the jurisdictions of cities/towns. Local regulations vary in contribution rates and reimbursement rates. The employee medical insurance policies separate working employees and retirees in terms of contribution rates as well as reimbursement amounts and covered services. Different policy settings under UEIMS and RUMIS contributed further to the complexity of the healthcare service regulations.

The newly established NHSA has ended the segmented administration status of the healthcare services. NHSA also paved the way for implementing a universal LTCI under one agency and close integration with the healthcare system. Whether the LTCI will develop into an independent social insurance or be a subdivision of the healthcare system has still not been confirmed. However, providing LTC to all elderly citizens has become an institutional goal.

The following analysis is based on the LTCI pilots. The background to the traditional policy arrangements might help to understand the differences between these pilots. All regional pilot LTC projects are based on their own social, economic, and demographic characteristics, as well as its social security policy developments. We summarize the basic features of three main areas: service model and corresponding benefits; source of funding; and recipients, eligibility, and current coverage. We end by estimating the national cost based on each pilot model to provide a range of the cost scenarios.

Service model and corresponding benefits

The LTC service model varies in each region and is very much determined by local government's initial motivation to launch such a program. The model is associated with its healthcare system, social security status for the disabled and elders, as well as the region's social and economic status. The services provided also vary. For example, whereas Qingdao provides quite a full range of LTC services, ranging from residential care to nursing homes, Shanghai and Nantong mainly offer home care packages (Nantong also provides cash payments to low-income family carers).

Qingdao pilot

In 2019, approximately 22% of Qingdao's population was aged 60 and above. Qingdao is one of the first cities to launch the LTCI program and its initial aim was to extend its medical services to home and residential places. There are four types of services covered by Qingdao's LTCI program, targeting different groups of people in need: hospital special care, nursing home care, home care, and mobile care.

Grades 2 and 3 hospitals provide "hospital special care" for people with very high medical needs but differ from acute hospital patients. The subsidy for hospital special care varies from RMB 180 to 210 (US$28–32) per day per bed depending on the grade of the hospital (for tracheotomy patients, the subsidy is RMB 300 (US$46) per day per bed). Primary medical institutions and qualified nursing homes can provide "nursing home care" to disabled LTC recipients. Their subsidy is RMB 65 (US$10) per day per bed. By 2016, about 18 public hospitals had set up geriatric service beds. The government has recently issued new regulations stating that by 2022, about 65% of comprehensive hospitals, rehabilitation hospitals, nursing homes, and primary care institutions would be elderly friendly institutions. Primary institutions would have 35% of total beds fulfil LTC purposes.

Home care and day care at community centres are mainly provided by private medical clinics developed with the help of the LTCI policy. Doctors, nurses, and carers provide services in the recipients' residential homes. The subsidy is RMB 50 (US$7.7) per day per recipient. The care is divided into two major categories: medical services and social daily care services. Nurses or doctors must provide at least four services per week in order to claim a full subsidy.

Mobile care, which is provided by qualified doctors and nurses, is only available to residents with irregular medical care needs at home. The subsidy, or annual fee, is RMB 3,500 (US$538) per person for employee basic medical insurance holders, RMB 3,000 (US$462) for university and high-grade residents' medical insurance holders and RMB 2,500 (US$385) for low-grade medical insurance holders.

Qingdao also provides social care to LTC recipients, but this is limited to UEBMI holders. Benefits vary from RMB 660/1050/1500 (US$102/162/231) per month depending on the disability levels of the recipient. All benefits require co-payment for out-of-pocket expenses, ranging from 10% to 20%.

At this stage, UEBMI members still receive higher benefits and lower co-pay ratios than that of RUMIS members in Qingdao, which is due to the different contribution amounts. In 2018, UEMIS contributes an average about RMB 3,900 (US$600), both from employees (9% of wage) and individuals (2%). The RUMIS-Low (including children) contributes RMB 260 (US$40)/year compared to RUMIS-High of RMB 390 (US$60) (university students counted as RUMIS-H paying only RMB 125 (US$19)); it is anticipated that most elders would choose RUMIS-High program. Table 3.1 summarizes the service types covered under the two member schemes.

Shanghai pilot

In 2019, the population aged 60 and above in Shanghai passed 35%. Shanghai had extended its medical services to home before the LTC pilot project started. The motivation and service model for Shanghai

Table 3.1 Service types for Urban Employee Basic Medical Insurance members (UEMIS), Residents High-contribution Medical Care members (RUMIS-High), and Residents Low-contribution Medical Care members (RUMIS-Low)

Health status	Service types	UEMIS	RUMIS-high	RUMIS-low
ADLs disabled	Hospital care	√	√	–
	Institutional care	√	√	–
	Home care	√	–	–
	Mobile care	√	√	√
Severe dementia	Long-term care	√	√	–
	Day care	√	–	–
	Respite care	√	√	–

was therefore focused on social care, rather than medical care from the very beginning. Shanghai provides three types of LTC services: home care, institutional care (in nursing homes), and hospital care.

Shanghai's home care model outlines 42 detailed services for its LTC recipients, covering medical as well as social care items. Elders who are eligible for grade 2 or 3 treatment are entitled to three hours of home care service per week, while those eligible for grades 4 and 5 treatment receive five and seven hours, respectively. For the service subsidy, the rate per hour is RMB 80 (US$12) for doctors, RMB 65 (US$10) for nurses, and RMB 40 (US$6) for carers (2019 rates, individual co-payment ratio is 10%). Nursing home recipients, according to the assessment grades, are entitled to a subsidy of RMB 20/25/30 (US$3/4/5) per day per bed (individual co-pay ratio is 15%). Hospital care is integrated with regulations of health care under the basic medical insurance schemes (BSHRSS-2018-No 36).

Based on the LTCI alone, nursing home recipients seem to receive less funds than home care recipients. This is partly due to the existence of nursing home subsidies from other government agencies (as explained above). Thus, home care is strongly encouraged as there is a bonus subsidy for eligible recipients: those assessed at level 5 or 6 (most severely disabled) who receive services for one to six months can either receive an extra hour's service per month, and two hours if receiving services for more than six months, or a cash subsidy of RMB 40 and 80 (US$6 and 12) per week, respectively.

Nantong pilot

Nantong is also considered to be an ageing city, with the population aged 60 and above exceeding 30%. Nantong implemented its LTCI program in 2015, and it provides nursing home care, as well as equipment leasing and daily provisions at a very low cost (An, Chen and Xiong 2017, He 2016).

The subsidy rate has increased dramatically since 2015. According to Document Nantong Medical Insurance (2020-13), the nursing home subsidy was RMB 60 (US$9) per person per day (with a co-payment of 40%) in the 2015 program but was increased to RMB 70 (US$11) per person per day (without any co-payment) in 2020. A cash subsidy of RMT 450 (US$69) per month is provided for home care, and in the case of severely disabled recipients, two to three instances of home services per week are also provided. Cash subsidies are not common practice in China, and Nantong is one of only four pilot programs offering cash payments. For home care and residential care, the government subsidizes necessary equipment while also providing goods consumed on a daily basis like adult nappies. In 2018, persons with a disability or dementia and eligible for home care were able to rent 6 types of assistive devices, including wheelchairs, nursing beds, and nursing robots at prices ranging from RMB 1 to RMB 10 (US$0.2–2) per day; they were also able to apply to purchase 15 types of assistive consumables, including diapers, nursing pads, toilet chairs, and walking aids at a price far below the market price.

The three cities represent typical LTC service models. The benefits in the three LTC models vary in subsidy values, and the models themselves are all changing rapidly to adjust to an ever-growing ageing population and corresponding costs. Most cities started their models by focusing on severely disabled beneficiaries and urban residents but are now expanding their coverage to include semi-dependent as well as rural residents.

Source of LTC insurance funding and recipients

The regional LTC programs were encouraged to be trialled in a pilot format without a centralized unified policy. It is understandable that there are various methods to integrate LTC into current medical care systems, as these systems continue to evolve to cope with future problems and challenges. Major funding sources include the medical insurance fund, welfare lottery fund, individual contributions, government transfers, and in a few cases, private company contributions. Typical LTC financing choices include taking a small portion of funds from the medical care system (like Shanghai); using parts of individual medical care accounts together with government subsidies, including the welfare lottery (like Qingdao); and, in other cases, an individual contribution is required together with the pooled medical care account fund transfer (like Nantong for RUMIS members). We will analyze each city as a typical pilot example.

Qingdao pilot

Qingdao has been reforming its LTC program since 2006, including its funding scheme. The current LTC financing mechanism, integrated into its major health insurance plans, is illustrated in Figure 3.1.

The LTCI in Qingdao has two accounts to cover two types of health insurance holders with different service types and co-payment ratios. According to Finance Yearbook of China 2018 (p. 208), the total LTCI expenditure was RMB 330 (US$51) million (including social care

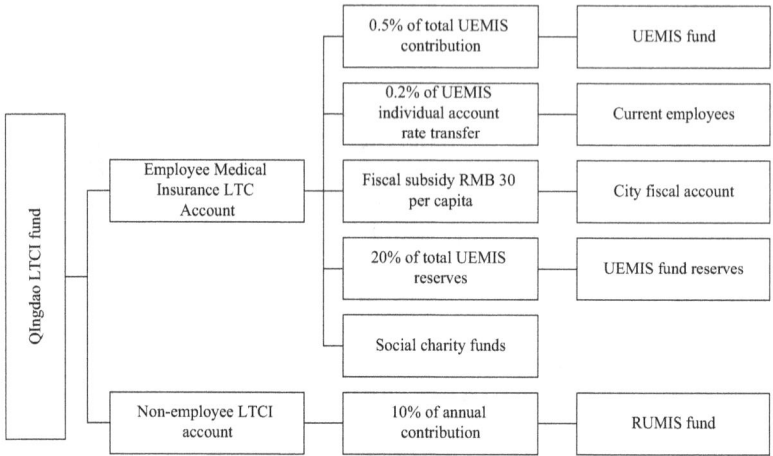

Figure 3.1 Qingdao LTCI accounts and funding structure

expenditure for employee medical insurance holders of about RMB 28.7 million (US$4.4 million)), which covers approximately 8.7 million residents in Qingdao, with 1.9 million aged 60 and above. According to Mi et al. (2018, p. 4), each member cost about RMB 40,000 (US$6,154) with average 53 months of length of stay, which indicates the estimated annual cost for 2015 Qingdao LTC recipients was about RMB 9,000 (US$1,385).

Shanghai pilot

Shanghai's current funding system is simple as it is fully funded by the medical insurance fund. The wage contribution of 1%, which is added to the employee medical insurance fund, is transferred directly to the LTCI fund. For urban and rural basic medical insurance holders, a slightly smaller amount is transferred to LTCI. The integrated LTCI covers all medical insurance holders, and all are entitled to the same services.

As stated in the previous section, historically, Shanghai has had subsidies for nursing home residents, which is part of the total LTC support. For year 2020, the total LTC expenditure in Shanghai reached RMB 3.8 billion (US$59 million) (including assessment fees). About 79% of the expenditure funded home care with the remaining funding nursing home institutions (Zhang and Yao 2022, p. 138).

The total number of recipients in Shanghai in 2020 was around 507,100, with 400,600 receiving home care services. The total registered population above age 60 was about 5.2 million, about 10% of the elders are LTCI recipients (Zhang and Yao 2022, p. 134).

Nantong pilot

The Nantong pilot is financed by multiple sources and is claimed to be dynamic (An, Cheng and Xiong 2017). Unlike Qingdao and Shanghai, individuals are required to contribute to their LTCI. The contribution for the LTCI is RMB 100 (US$15) per person, of which the government fiscal transfer is RMB 40 (US$6); basic medical insurance is RMB 30 (US$4.6), and the individual pays RMB 30 (US$4.6). The welfare lottery and other charity funds are also used for funding when needed.

By the end of July 2017, Nantong's LTCI expenditure was reported to be RMB 13 million (US$2 million), covering 3,767 recipients. The Jiangsu Province, where Nantong is situated, expanded its pilot LTCI to 7 cities. By the end of 2019, the LTCI covered about 7.15 million citizens, with 25,727 benefit recipients. Approximately 84% of recipients received home care and the remainder received institutional care. According to China Daily Newspaper on May 14, 2021, it was reported that about 19% of long-stay hospital patients were transferred to LTC institutions by the end of October 2019.

Eligibility and current coverage

Eligibility and its associated benefits may determine the total cost of a LTC system. Most pilot LTCI programs in China started with severely disabled elders and generally covered employee medical insurance holders. This is because social support services for severely disabled elders are paramount, and employee medical insurers have a surplus in their medical insurance funds. Therefore, eligibility has been evolving with greater demand and expansion of the LTCI coverage.

Qingdao pilot

Initially, the Qingdao pilot covered employee medical insurance holders in urban areas. Eligibility criteria came from the Barthel index with ten assistant daily livings and mini-mental state examination assessments (MMSE) for cognitive impairment. A person is entitled to receive LTCI benefits if they score 60 or below, with a score of 100 representing a fully independent person. This assessment is accompanied by a professional medical report of the person's health status.

Current eligible recipients are divided into four levels: levels 3–5 disabilities with ADLs plus medical conditions, and a severe dementia level (social care benefits equivalent to level 5 disability recipients). The assessment procedure is conducted by third parties through tender, and these are currently operated by commercial insurance companies.

The average number of recipients from 2015 to 2017 was about 20,000 in Qingdao, which is about 1% of the population aged 60 and above.

Shanghai pilot

Shanghai has a unique assessment system based on applicants' disability status, disease status, and care conditions. The applicants also need to be aged 60 or above. Assessment results are divided into 6 care levels, from levels 1 to 6. Level 1 is not entitled to any LTC service, while levels 2–6 are entitled to varying levels of support. For example, level 2 receives three hours of home care per week, and level 6 receives seven hours.

Assessments are conducted by qualified agencies. The assessment fee is RMB 200 per person, with individuals paying 20% and the remainder is covered by the LTCI fund. Shanghai launched LTCI in 2018 and by 2020, there had been about half million LTC recipients, with an annual approximate cost of around RMB 3,000 per person. The beneficiary rates using Shanghai's eligibility are much higher than Qingdao, reaching about 10% of citizens aged 60 and above.

Nantong pilot

Like Qingdao, Nantong also entrusted commercial insurance companies to conduct its assessments of eligible recipients. The criteria are mainly based on the Barthel Index table. While the initial pilot only applied to severely disabled persons (with a Barthel score of less than 40), the program has gradually expanded to semi-disabled (with a score of 41–50 out of 100). The assessment is accompanied by medical records and personal identification. Neighbours would also be asked about the applicants' disability status.

Nantong has a public announcement system for all eligible recipients, which is open for about one week. Anyone who has a dispute can contact the service centre. In principle, all recipients are reassessed every two years.

The average cost for each eligible recipient is approximately RMB 4,270 (UDS 657) per year. In terms of coverage, the policy has gradually been extended to cover semi-disabled elderly citizens, and it was claimed by a total of 25,725 recipients by September 2020, according to

Bin Zhang, director of Nantong Municipal Medical Security Bureau in Nantong's LTC insurance Five-Year Anniversary Press conference. It is unclear how many existing beneficiaries there were in 2019–2020, but we assume that 1% of the 2.3 million aged 60 and above in Nantong were covered.

Estimating future national LTC insurance costs

The LTCI pilot programs currently operating in China correspond to different demographic and economic development stages. The Qingdao, Shanghai, and Nantong models are all situated in developed areas. While China's GDP per capita was RMB 64,609 (US$9,940) in 2019, the three cities reached above RMB 110,000 (US$17,077) two years ago, with Shanghai and Qingdao being twice the average national level. The three cities are also advanced in ageing. To some extent, the pilots in these cities provide an indication of a future policy framework for LTC in China.

This chapter will use the three cities' operational data to estimate the national cost of a unified LTCI, based on various eligibility criteria and service models. These may also be applicable to other areas or cities in different stages.

We estimate the individual annual service price based on the current subsidy standards in the three cities. Shanghai is calculated based on five hours of service visits per week at an average of RMB 65 (US$10) per visit, which amounts to a cost of RMB 16,900 (US$2,600) per person; Qingdao is based on recipients receiving 10% hospital special care and 90% home care, which amounts to RMB 16,426 (US$2,527) per year (hospital care at RMB 200 (US$31) per day, and home care at RMB 65 (US$10), three times per week); and Nantong is estimated at RMB 14,880 (US$2,289) per year based on 15% institutional care and at RMB 2,100 (US$323) per month for 85% home care. Nantong's home care is calculated at RMB 450 (US$69) per month cash plus RMB 90 (US$15) per week service; and an additional RMB 4,800 (US$738) of home care expenditure is assumed for its rental equipment and consumable assistive devices supplies.

Table 3.2 estimates the current costs based on the existing practices of the three cities, extending these to a national level. It also provides a national estimate based on 10% of people aged 60 and above being entitled to services, using current rates. Costs include individual co-payments (in Shanghai's case).

Shanghai has extended its services relatively comprehensively covering the majority of people aged 60 and above who need support. Both Qingdao and Nantong continue to primarily target severely disabled

Table 3.2 LTC expenditure based on three cities' practice and pricing
mechanism

	Shanghai	Qingdao	Nantong
Eligible rate (% of 60+)	10.0%	1.0%	1.0%
Average benefit (RMB per year)	16,900	16,426	14,880
GDP pc 2019[*] (RMB/USD)	135,000/20,726	135,202/20,800	115,359/17,747
Benefit as % of GDP pc	12.5%	12.1%	12.9%
National estimate (% GDP)	0.48%	0.05%	0.05%
If 10% of 60+ covered nationally	0.2%	0.2%	0.2%

[*]Information of GDP per capita for three cities is from various local statistics bureau
websites.

cohorts and the main difference in total expenditure of the LTCI programs lies in the coverage rate.

The pilot programs also confirm that for other areas where LTCI is
not implemented, a starting cost of 0.05% of the local GDP is feasible.
In all three cases, the actual expenditure to date is much less than the
local GDP ratio as estimated in Table 3.2. This is partly because we
estimate according to the severely disabled benefit and do not consider any reduction in expenditure from mildly disabled recipients. We
do not exclude the out-of-pocket payments either, which are in some
instances required by individuals.

This affordable starting cost would greatly improve the quality of
life of both the carers and disabled elders in the region. With the current design structure, even a moderate coverage of 10% of residents
aged 60 and above would only cost about 0.2% of GDP with the current
price settings. This is much lower than the average OECD countries
and indicates that more service provisions for the elderly are expected.

Labour force and economic contribution

The LTCI also promotes new job opportunities in the pilot cities.
Zhang (2020) reported that about 20,000 new jobs were added in
Qingdao because of the LTCI implementation; Shanghai registered
63,000 service personnel for LTC; and Nantong registered over 10,000
service personnel.

We use Qingdao and Shanghai as examples of LTCI's impact on the
labour force and employment opportunities. As mentioned earlier, Qingdao's expenditure on LTC was RMB 330 million (US$51 million) in 2018,

Table 3.3 Shanghai and Qingdao's LTC insurance impact on job
opportunities and economic contributions

	Salary (RMB)	Labour force	Total expenditure (RMB million)	LTCI cost (RMB million)	Total expl LTCI cost ratio
Shanghai	80,134	63,000	5,048	3,800	1.3
Qingdao	57,988	20,000	1,160	330	3.5

and Shanghai's expenditure was RMB 3.8 billion (US$5,846 million) in 2020. According to the Bureau of Statistics website information, an average salary for the private sector in Shanghai was RMB 80,134 (US$12,328) in 2020, and in 2018 Qingdao, it was RMB 57,988 (US$8,921). Table 3.3 summarizes the effect of LTCI on new jobs and associated ratios.

If LTCI triggers the creation of new jobs, with some government subsidy, then we could be interpreted in a way that every dollar spent on LTCI generates 3.5 dollar worth of wages in new employment in Qingdao. The economic contribution by such an insurance seems to be reasonably high.

The analysis provides an indication of the broader economic impact of a LTCI. The introduction of an LTCI seems not only to meet the demand for care by an increasingly ageing population, but also to create new job opportunities and therefore also offer economic benefits. To put it another way, the current LTCI expenditure is about 0.03% of the local GDP for both cities, but the LTC-generated employment is about 0.4% for Shanghai and 0.2% for Qingdao as a proportion of total employees.

Another method of analysis combines the total health cost, including medical care and LTC, and tests if there is a substitutional effect of LTC to medical care. One of the results from Qingdao by primary research concludes that

the total cost to the government-subsidized medical insurance decreases by around RMB 7918 (US$1,218) per recipient. The cost to the individual decreases by around RMB 2324 (US$358) per recipient. Thus, netting a decrease of RMB 10,242 (US$1,576) in total expenditure. Furthermore, — that there is a 12% reduction in inpatient service after a recipient participates in the pilot.

(Lu et al. 2020)

Feng, Wang and Yu (2020) had similar results using the Shanghai model. Their study found that every extra one unit dollar spent on LTCI will generate a decrease of 8.6 unit in healthcare insurance expenditure. This is a greater effect on aggregated savings. As for Nantong, Liu (2020) reported that during the three-year trial period of the LTCI program, the medical care expenditure for LTC recipients reduced to RMB 99.7 million (US$15.3 million) from RMB 162 (US$25) million.

The substitutional effect of LTCI to medical care insurance is partly derived from the so called "social hospitalization", where older citizens with morbidities stay in hospitals as if they were nursing homes. This is true if there is no LTC facility arrangement, and there is a profit-driven motivation for hospitals to keep patients. In this sense, the LTCI, if implemented at an early stage, can control the social hospitalization phenomenon.

Policy indications and discussion

Qingdao was one of the first pilots to launch a regional LTCI in 2012 and it has undergone several major policy reforms since its first trial. A national unified LTC policy is yet to be launched and will probably not be available for a few years. However, the framework is likely to be similar to the three models we have discussed.

For regions where medical insurance has not extended to home or residential places as in Qingdao, a sensible option is to start the LTC system by primarily detaching the LTC recipients from hospital services (including clinic patients in the major hospitals). This will reallocate the medical services more effectively and at the same time, may even reduce aggregated costs (LTC and health care combined).

Once primary care is developed in communities along with the promotion of LTCI, more resources could be moved to social care and gradually integrated with health care. For regions with healthcare systems already extended to home and residential places (e.g., Shanghai), designing a social care system that is perhaps a home care-biased system is more logical. This will also make it easier to provide equal care to all residents, regardless of their healthcare coverage. Another method is to provide a cash subsidy, in addition to equipment and facility provisions, such as an informal care supplement model like Nantong. This is a different approach and can be exercised to enhance the traditional family care.

Several challenges remain for China to have a unified policy scenario. One possibility is that a regionally initiated pattern could be continued for a long period of time. This is partly due to the difficulty in converging China's unbalanced social and economic development in the near future. Other challenges for a nationally unified system include the treatment of migrant populations, different regional population ageing structures, as well as the integration of existing policies for age pension, health, disability, and other welfare systems.

If the policy does intend to be unified, then a lower benefit level would be expected given the ageing trajectory and conservative public budget. If that is the case, commercial LTCI might be introduced for developed areas to cover the extra cost in those regions. It would induce a new market of LTCI demand and could be interesting to follow.

However, one essential part of the LTC policy that could be unified first is the assessment criteria for LTC recipients. Currently, there are several assessment tools in different regions. Assessment teams need to be standardized and professionally trained and supervised. Protocols for eligibility, assessment, service provider qualifications, service quality, and safety and other related issues need to be regulated and monitored through a national framework or guidelines. Designated agencies for these regulations and practices also need to be specified or established together with a pricing guideline. Progress has been made to unify the assessment criteria as the first step to a unified policy with the establishment NHSA. In August 2021, a major document on LTCI was issued: Notice from the Office of the NHSA and the General Office of the MCA on Issuing the "Long-term Care Disability Level Assessment Standard (Trial)" (Doc. 2021-No.37). This document lists the matrix of assessment tools and defines five levels of disability for LTCI practice: mild level, moderate level, severe level I, severe level II, and severe level III. The assessment tool combines activities in daily living (ADLs), cognitive ability, sensory, and communication ability. The associated services and benefits to the various disability levels will be defined by local governments. After a decade of pilot programs in China, this is the first document which defines national standards of eligibility for LTC services with universal assessment criteria.

The demand for LTC in China has only recently begun. Several research projects have explored the future demand for LTC in China. For example, Lu, Liu and Yang (2017) report that the demand for LTC among people aged 60 and above will be about 12.9% in 2030, and 11.4% in 2050 (considering the health improvement for elders). Together with the population forecast by Lu and Piggott (2014), this will translate to about 48 and 58 million people respectively. Covering such a large cohort's LTC demand is likely to be challenging, and priorities are needed. If only disabled older citizens with ADLs are covered, the demand would be reduced by 40–50% of the total (Lu and Piggott 2014).

Pilot programs are prudent to start with even more strict eligibility criteria. They can be of reference to regions which are yet to launch such a plan, or to other developing countries which may experience similar trajectories.

The LTCI scheme in China is only in its early phases and will not mature for many years to come. Whether LTC in China becomes an independent social insurance or a universal social security program with basic benefits, or both, is still under discussion. To separate different income groups with differentiated demands, a voluntary commercial insurance on top of a universal safety net type of social program (or insurance) seems more feasible. Given current vital regional differences, introducing designing a formal national LTCI policy is not going to be an easy task. Most of the pilot programs have been initiated in developed areas, with benefits limited to the most severely disabled elders (recipients), and this paves the way ahead. Future developments will focus on an extension of services to the needs of all older citizens.

Future challenges

With a rapidly growing demand in the future, several challenges need to be overcome to ensure a successful LTC policy. These include the integration of formal and informal care, service expansion to dementia care, as well as supervision of the LTC policy's sustainability, efficiency, equality, and effectiveness both in social and economic circumstances.

In most developed countries with a sophisticated LTC system, informal care still plays a major role in caring for the elderly. A recent European LTC study (Bonsang 2009) suggests that informal care is an effective substitute for LTC as long as the needs of the elderly are low and only in need of an unskilled type of care. The study indicates that any policy encouraging informal care to decrease LTC expenditures should take the level of care into account to assess its effectiveness. The developed world's comparatively mature LTC policy findings are important to China's policy agenda into the future. Social LTC will not substitute family based informal care; rather, it will offer high-care support by skilled staff.

An important shortfall in the policy coverage is dementia care, which is under-explored in current pilot programs in China. Dementia care is a key part of the demand for LTC, especially for institutional care. In Australia, according to AIHW (2021) report, more than half of the residential care recipients suffer from dementia. The three highlighted pilots in China have prioritized their service target to the severely disabled elderly with ADLs difficulties, and seemingly only Qingdao included dementia patients in the eligibility criteria. World Alzheimer Report 2016 (Prince et al. 2016) estimated that by 2030, there will be about 16 million people with dementia in China. In Europe, the cost of caring for people with dementia is reported to be about €28,000 (US$34,720) (in 2005) per year per capita (Jönsson and Wimo 2009). This will translate into a huge financial challenge to the future Chinese LTCI system. For China to cope with, this trajectory requires sustainable strategies.

So far, the three pilot programs in China have generated quite similar cost structures per recipient, which confirms the feasibility of these practices. Though the cost is very low compared to developed countries, the pilot programs are only targeting the cohorts with the most critical needs. It is also assumed that a greater expansion of benefits is expected in the future, resulting in a higher cost structure. The demand for coverage expansion (including dementia care), together with the service expansion, will accelerate the challenge of a sustainable policy design.

We have briefly discussed the impact of an LTCI program on the labour force in terms of new employment opportunities. The results seem to be relatively positive. With more service products and more demand for social assistance in LTC, the demand for human resources in the LTC field will grow rapidly. While formal LTC is costly in nature, it can result in economic efficiency when carefully designed. Regular evaluation of the economic efficiency as well as equality and effectiveness in social terms will be another policy challenge.

The assessment standardization may be the first step for a unified national system; however, heterogeneity in regional social and economic status implies that an LTCI might follow the healthcare insurance, which in that case would be under regional operation, with portable rights using a national platform. At this stage, disability benefits offered by the CDPF and senior subsidies provided by MCA are yet to be merged into a LTCI. LTCI is far from mature in China, with benefit disparities in both inter- and intro-regions. However, the pilots introduced in this chapter might shed some light on the future development of the policy and operational framework of a LTCI, both for domestic use and other developing countries.

References

An, P.P., Chen, N. and Xiong, B., 2017. System practice, experience and trends on the long-term care insurance of China: based on a comparative study of Qingdao model and Nantong model. *Chinese Journal of Health Policy*, *10*(8), pp. 1–6.

Australian Institute of Health and Welfare (AIHW), 2021. Web report on "Population health impacts of dementia", via Dementia in Australia, Population health impacts of dementia – Australian Institute of Health and Welfare (aihw.gov.au).

Bloom, D.E., Chatterji, S., Kowal, P., Lloyd-Sherlock, P., McKee, M., Rechel, B., Rosenberg, L. and Smith, J.P., 2015. Macroeconomic implications of population ageing and selected policy responses. *The Lancet, 385*(9968), pp. 649–657.

Blumenthal, D. and Hsiao, W., 2005. Privatization and its discontents—the evolving Chinese health care system. *New England Journal of Medicine, 353*(11), pp. 1165–1170.

Blumenthal, D. and Hsiao, W., 2015. Lessons from the East—China's rapidly evolving health care system. *New England Journal of Medicine, 372*(14), pp. 1281–1285.

Bonsang, E., 2009. Does informal care from children to their elderly parents substitute for formal care in Europe?. *Journal of Health Economics, 28*(1), pp. 143–154.

Bureau of Shanghai Huma Resources and Social Security (BSHRSS-2018-No 36), 2018. Notice to Shanghai long-term care insurance community, home care and residential institutional care service regulations, via 关于印发《上海市长期护理保险社区居家和养老机构护理服务规程（试行）》的通知_医疗保险_上海市人力资源和社会保障局 (sh.gov.cn).

China State Finance Magazine, 2019. Finance Yearbook of China 2018.

Feng, J., Wang, Z. and Yu, Y., 2020. Does long-term care insurance reduce hospital utilization and medical expenditures? Evidence from China. *Social Science & Medicine, 258*, p. 113081. DOI: 10.1016/j.socscimed.2020.113081.

Glinskaya, E. and Feng, Z., 2018. *Options for aged care in China: Building an efficient and sustainable aged care system.* World Bank Publications.

Jönsson, L. and Wimo, A., 2009. The cost of dementia in Europe. *Pharmacoeconomics, 27*(5), pp. 391–403.

He, T.T., 2016. Disclose the first long-term care insurance pilot city. *Nantong Sample, Architecture Knowledge*, (12), pp. 52–53.

Hu, B., 2019. Projecting future demand for informal care among older people in China: the road towards a sustainable long-term care system. *Health Economics, Policy and Law, 14*(1), pp. 61–81.

Liu, H.B., 2020. Long-term care insurance helps to build age friendly society, China Finance (in Chinese), Vol 6, via. 《中国金融》 | 长护险助力老龄友好型社会建设_手机新浪网 (sina.cn).

Lu, B. and Piggott, J., 2014. Meeting the migrant pension challenge in China. *CESifo Economic Studies*, June. DOI:10.1093/cesifo/ifu017

Lu, B., Liu, X. and Yang, M.X., 2017. A budget proposal for China's public long term care policy. *Journal of Aging and Social Policy, 29*(1) pp. 84–103. DOI:10.1080/08959420.2016.1187058

Lu, B., Liu, X., Lim, J. and Yang, M., 2019. Changes in the morbidity prevalence and morbidity-free life expectancy of the elderly population in China from 2000 to 2010. *The Journal of the Economics of Ageing, 13*, pp. 113–121.

Lu, B., Mi, H., Yan, G., Lim, J.K. and Feng, G., 2020. Substitutional effect of long-term care to hospital inpatient care? *China Economic Review, 62.* DOI: 10.1016/j.chieco.2020.101466.

Mi, H., Fan, X., Lu, B., Cai, L. and Piggott, J., 2020. Preparing for population ageing: estimating the cost of formal aged care in China. *The Journal of the Economics of Ageing, 17.* DOI: 10.1016/j.jeoa.2018.12.002.

Ministry of Civil Affairs (MCA) and Ministry of Finance (MOF), 2016. "Notice to support pilot programs of home care and communities long-term care service reforms through central funding" (Document 200), via http://www.moe.gov.cn/s78/A24/A24_zcwj/201607/t20160726_272958.html

Ministry of Civil Affairs (MCA) and National Development and Reform Committee (NDRC), 2021. The 14th Five Years Civil Affairs and Development Plan, via 1602721650061.pdf (mca.gov.cn).MOHRSS (Ministry of Human Resources and Social Security, 2016. guidelines for establishing long-term care insurance system pilots by MOHRSS" (Document 2016-80), via 人力资源社会保障部办公厅关于开展长期护理保险制度试点的指导意见 (mohrss.gov.cn).

National Healthcare Security Administration of the PRC (NHSA), 2021. Quick report on 2020 Medical Protection Development Statistics, 我国基本医保参保覆盖面稳定在95%以上_滚动新闻_中国政府网 (www.gov.cn)Office of Ministry of Civil Affairs (MCA), Notice No 139, 2020, via 1602721650061.pdf (mca.gov.cn).

Office of the NHSA and the General Office of the MCA (Doc. 2021-No.37), 2021. Long-term care disability level assessment standard (Trial), 国家医保局办公室 民政部办公厅关于印发《长期护理失能等级评估标准（试行）》的通知_其他_中国政府网 (www.gov.cn).

Prince, M., Comas-Herrera, A., Knapp, M., Guerchet, M. and Karagiannidou, M., 2016. World Alzheimer report 2016: improving healthcare for people living with dementia: coverage, quality and costs now and in the future. London: Alzheimer's Disease International.

Zhang, J., 2020. Achievements, problems and suggestions of china long-term care insurance pilot program, China Center for International Economic Exchanges: 我国长期护理保险制度试点成效、问题和建议 - 产业经济 - 中国国际经济交流中心 (cciee.org.cn).

Zhang, T. and Yao, J.W., 2022. Study on long-term care insurance fund expenditure based on actuarial model-taking shanghai as an example. *Advances in Applied Mathematics, 11*(2), pp. 133–140, published online January 2022 in Hans. http://www.hanspub.org/journal/aam. DOI:10.12677/aam.2022.111019

4 Public long-term care in Thailand

Nalinee N. Chuakhamfoo, Vasoontara S. Yiengprugsawan, and Supasit Pannarunothai

Background

As of early 2022, the total population of Thailand was approximately 66.8 million people (Institute for Population and Social Research of Mahidol University, 2022). The United Nations World Population Prospects 2019 estimate that, currently, 19% of Thailand's total population is aged 60 years and over, or about 13.4 million people. Thailand's society is ageing and will be a superaged society by 2035, with 30% of the population aged 60 and over, or about 21 million people compared to about 48.6 million people aged 0–59 years old (United Nations 2019a). Hence, as the population ages, the ageing dependency ratio (the estimation of the ratio of population, considering people aged 65 and over per 100 people aged 25–64 in Thailand) increases over time (see Figure 4.1) (United Nations, 2019b). The changing face of the country's economy, society, and public health system in Thailand has affected the size, structure, and relationship patterns in families and communities. Extended families have been shrinking, while nuclear families have been increasing over time. Thailand has been facing a decreasing fertility rate since 1965, and this trend is continuing (see Figure 4.2). Furthermore, urbanisation has grown and female education has continued to improve. As children enter adulthood and leave home, the empty-nest syndrome is also increasing. In addition, the percentage of elderly who live alone has increased from 3.6% in 1994 (National Statistical Office of Thailand, 2002) to 12.4% in 2020 (Institute for Population and Social Research of Mahidol University, 2021). Thus, the culture of informal aged care in the family, which has been the mainstream in the past, has now decreased.

Similar to other Asian countries, the main long-term care (LTC) providers for the Thai elderly have been family members. Based on piety values, which are part of Asian countries' culture, female family

DOI: 10.4324/9781003131373-4

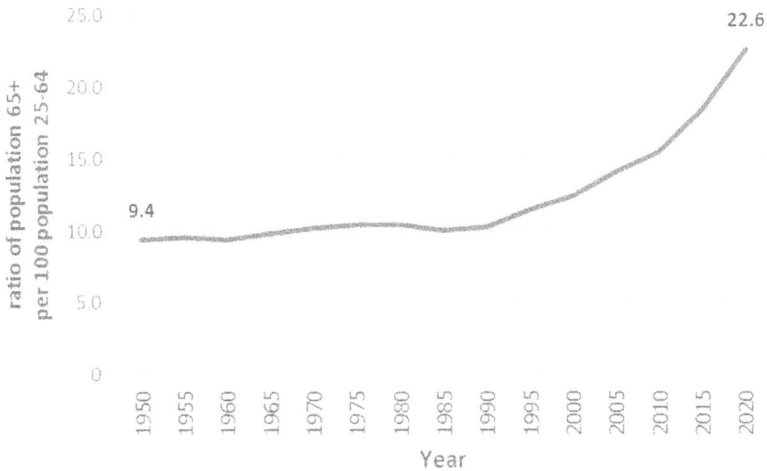

Figure 4.1 The estimation of old-age dependency ratio in Thailand from 1960
to 2020
Source: United Nations, Department of Economic and Social Affairs, Population Division, 2019.

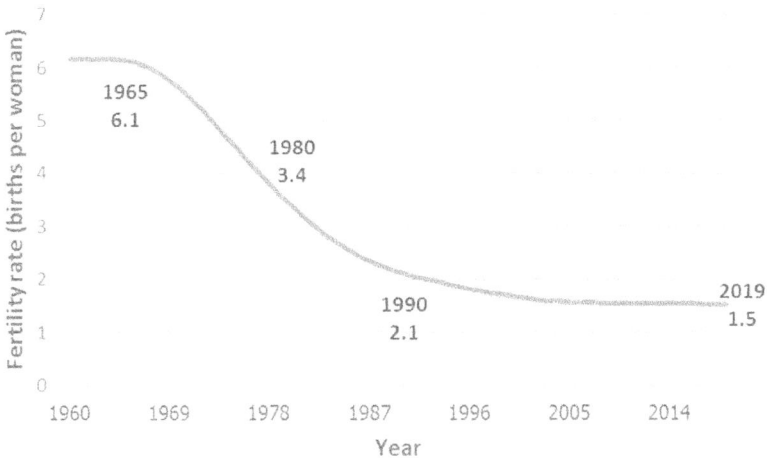

Figure 4.2 Fertility rate in Thailand from 1960 to 2019
Source: World Bank, 2019.

members are responsible for the care of the elderly. Lee (2012) found that 43.4% of Thai families preferred the daughter as a caregiver, compared to 14.2% in Japan, and 6.9% in Korea (Lee, 2012). However, the potential of family members as the main caregivers in the eastern world has been declining because of urbanisation and a greater emphasis on the nuclear family. Thailand has an LTC system which relies on the family member(s) as unpaid caregiver(s). Since the 1980s, however, the female population in Thailand has had a greater opportunity to complete higher levels of education. UNESCO figures show that the percentage of females aged 25 and over who completed their upper secondary school as 4.1% in 1980, 21.5% in 2004, and 35.6% in 2019 (UNESCO Institute for Statistics, 2021). This affects the norm that women should be the housekeeper and the main caregiver for the children and elderly in the household. The number of unpaid caregivers is therefore diminishing in Thai society. Moreover, when comparing the proportion of the working-age population (population aged 15–64) per elderly (population aged 65 and over), it was found that in 2016, there were 6.5 working-age people per 1 elderly. However, it is estimated that this number will decline and there will only be 3.4, 2.3, and 2.0 working-age people per elderly in 2030, 2040, and 2050, respectively (United Nations, 2019b).

Projection and long-term care needs in Thailand

Prasitsiriphon et al. (2013) examined the cost modelling scenarios and projected that based on the universal approach to LTC, the total cost for moderate and severe cases in Thailand may reach about US$1685.6 million in 2022 (Prasitsiriphon et al., 2013). Ageing is generally associated with limitations in performing activities of daily living (Asian Development Bank, 2020) and as the number of elderly increases, Prasitsiriphon et al. found that the demand for LTC services will be about 360,000 people in 2022 compared with 220,000 people in 2010 because of the increased number of elderly suffering from severe disability (Prasitsiriphon et al., 2014). A study by the Economic Research Institute for ASEAN and East Asia (ERIA) investigated the need for LTC services and found that the number of people in Thailand needing LTC services will continue to increase over time, from about 296,000 people in 2015 to 378,000 people in 2020, and it is estimated that this number will be more than a million in 2045 (Economic Research Institute for ASEAN and East Asia, 2019). The National Statistical Office of Thailand conducted a survey in 2017 which found that most of the elderly reported that they did not have a caregiver, and more than

Table 4.1 The number of elderly with/without a caregiver supporting with activities of daily living

Caregiver situation in 2017	The number of elderly	Percentage
Did not have a caregiver	9,755,298	86.24
Need a caregiver(s)	928,400	8.21
Had a caregiver(s)	17,293	0.15

Source: The National Statistical Office of Thailand, Survey of Older Persons (2018).

0.9 million of the elderly reported they need at least one caregiver (National Statistical Office of Thailand, 2018) (Table 4.1).

Clearly, Thailand is facing the ageing society phenomenon. The country's epidemiological changes have seen an increase in the number of people suffering from chronic non-communicable diseases (NCDs). However since 2020, with the whole world facing the COVID-19 pandemic, the challenges of emerging infectious diseases and the burden of NCDs in older persons engage in more online self-care programs and on-site vaccination (World Health Organization, 2020a). The working sector and the general public were concerned when the number of confirmed COVID-19 cases was rising in Thailand. The ageing population was identified as being at greater risk of severe illness compared with people in the working age group. There was broad concern among providers, purchasers, and the public over resources and supplies needed in the care of COVID-19 infected patients.

As the elderly with NCDs need regular care, they also tend to be at a greater risk of becoming severely ill from COVID-19 (World Health Organization, 2020b). The LTC system was affected by this situation and both urban and rural communities. Due to the COVID-19 situation, the LTC system in the post-pandemic era may change in terms of its care provision, resource allocation, and administrative arrangements (Institute for Population and Social Research of Mahidol University, 2021; Kaufman et al., 2011; Moroz et al., 2021; Office of the National Economic and Social Development Council, 2013; Wongtanasarasin et al., 2021).

National policy for older persons

Thailand has defined the elderly as persons of Thai nationality aged 60 and over (Elderly Person Act B.E. 2546, 2003). While focusing on LTC in this chapter, we refer to the care for persons aged 60 and over who need ongoing care for more than 6 months as they are unable to perform their daily living activities independently due to limited physical or cognitive functional status. Thus, the elderly with dependent functional status, which we currently define as the elderly who need LTC , might be included in the same group as the group defined as the elderly in Thailand.

Thailand launched the "Development of the First National Long-term Plan of Action for the Elderly" in 1982, which was part of the 1982–2001 plan. At that time, LTC in Thailand was not well-known nor well-defined and instead included all elderly in Thailand. The plan was intended as a guideline for aged care with comprehensive aspects such as health, education, social security, culture, and welfare (Jitapunkul & Wivatvanit, 2008).

This national plan reflects the norms of Thai society from the last 40 years which stipulate that the population itself should take care of the elderly. Private organisations and non-governmental organisations such as religious organisations should act as supporters or providers of social activities for older persons. Social support from the government was in the form of social welfare, which was an ongoing challenge in terms of appropriate delivery (Figure 4.3).

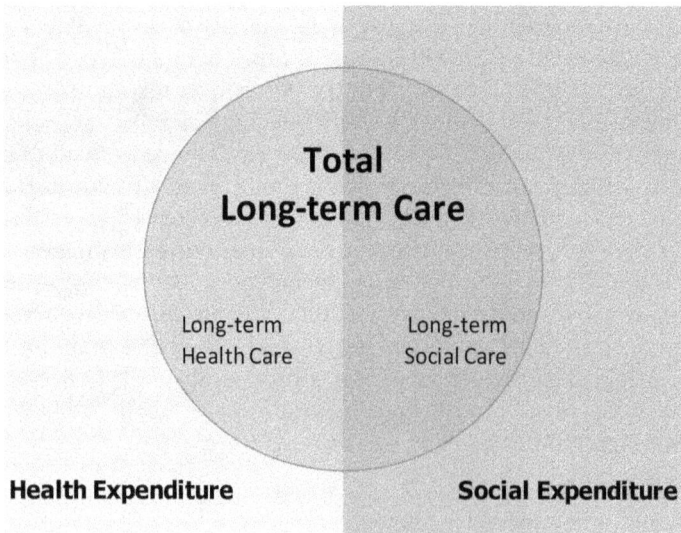

Total
Long-term Care

Long-term
Health Care

Long-term
Social Care

Health Expenditure   **Social Expenditure**

Figure 4.3 Long-term care within the Health and Social Sectors
Source: Recreate by authors based on OECD (2007) Conceptual Framework and Methods for Analysis of Data Sources for Long-Term Care Expenditure.

Focusing on the social services dimension in LTC, in the 1980s, Thailand was in the beginning phase of urbanisation. The labour force started to move to urban areas to work affecting the social structure in the rural areas. The rural population was about 87.5% in 1960 and it has since then decreased to close to 50% in 2020 (Goldstein, 1971; The Asian Population and Development Association, 1995; United Nations, 2018). As in the past, most of the elderly in Thailand live in rural areas and are therefore at risk of living alone or separated from their adult children due to this change in the social structure. At the time of the Development of the First National Long-term Plan of Action for the Elderly, there was no legal protection for the elderly in Thailand in terms of social welfare provision. The government provided limited benefits to very select target groups such as females aged 60 and over, and males aged 65 and over, who were suffering poverty, neglection, or were not able to be appropriately cared for by family members (Buracom, 2011). However, the national policy at that time did not offer any monthly allowances for an elderly person who had not been a former civil servant. Most of the elderly in Thailand did not receive a monthly allowance from the government during the 1980s. The benefits at that time tended to be for social aid (e.g. disabled, low-income, or no family members) instead of social welfare. The government has, however, been providing government shelters for the dependent elderly since 1953 (Jitapunkul & Chayovan, 2001).

The first governmental welfare institution was set up in 1933. The main mission for the government shelter, however, was social support rather than healthcare support as the responsible agency was the Public Welfare Department. This was despite the fact that most dependent elderly have age-related health problems. Thus, the government shelter may not have provided essential care for these elderly. The Sports Organization of Thailand was responsible for the health promotion program for both physical and mental health while the Buddhist temples supported the needs for formal and informal education, as well as psychological and social support in the community.

Thailand's past long-term health care can be divided into three phases. The first phase was from 1975 to 1991, the second phase was from 1992 to 2001, and the third phase, which preceded the current LTC provisions, was from 2002 to 2012. The first phase began with the Ministry of Public Health trying to scale up the district health system. A low-income scheme was launched to provide free medical care for low-income households, children, the disabled, and the elderly. At that time, general hospitals, located throughout the country in most provinces, attempted to set up geriatric care units. Thus, in 1978, the primary healthcare policy was launched and the Village Health Volunteers (VHV) became the main informal providers in the primary healthcare context from that time. Even now, the VHV system is one of the great success stories in the Thai health system. In 1980, the Special Geriatric Health Service Program was launched in Bangkok. The program mainly focused on developing human resources for aged care. In 1981, the National Committee on Coordination of Health Care for the Elderly was established (Monkhlung et al., 2016). The committee's mission was to plan and coordinate the health services for the elderly as well as liaising with international organisations such as the World Health Organization. This phase sets the foundation for Thailand's current LTC system through the well-structured primary healthcare units which can be found across the country.

The second phase began in 1992 with the publication the "Essence of Long-term Policies and Measures for the Elderly". It covered the years from 1992 to 2011 and it encouraged community care. As Thailand launches a new National Economic and Social Development Plan every five years, this period also covered the Eighth National Economic and Social Development Plan (1997–2001). According to the plan, the poor or neglected elderly should be entitled to free medical services and transportation fees. The plan also recommended that private hospitals, private entities, and community and religious organisations have a role in supporting the elderly.

The second National Plan for The Elderly 2002–2021 stated that the elderly are not a vulnerable group nor a burden to the Thai society. The benefit packages provided to the elderly should provide sufficient and appropriate care. This National Plan for the Elderly involved a shift from previous plans in that it advocated for health security and health promotion for the elderly. This plan signalled the beginning of a LTC policy in the Thai system as it referred to developing long-term community-based care including health as well as social services. The elderly in the community suffering from chronic diseases were included in the LTC group and the volunteers had the support from the government to provide basic services in the community. The local administration organisations had a greater role in community care from that period onwards.

In the third phase, 2002–2012, the National Health Security Office (NHSO) launched the Universal Health Coverage (UHC) scheme. Since implementing the UHC in 2002, Thailand found that it covered more than 72% of the total population (Sumriddetchkajorn et al., 2019). The UHC was seen as the foundation for the Thai LTC system, enabling it to grow as demand grows. However, a LTC system should include both health and social aspects. While the health sectors offer quality health services, there is also a need for social services. LTC systems in Thailand are public domain-driven and mostly rely on the UHC system. The UHC has led to three key achievements—increased population cover, expansion of services, and reduced financial risk. This is primarily due to the infrastructure at the district level which has continued to develop since 1970 resulting in a strong foundation for primary health care.

Until 2012, LTC in Thailand was not seen as a system or concept; only some services related to LTC services such as the home visiting program by primary healthcare providers. The primary healthcare centres were changed to be Subdistrict Health Promoting Hospitals which are all well-located in every subdistrict of the country. Primary health care has been the main LTC service provider since 2006 (see Case study 1); however, concrete financial support programs were not yet established at that time. Health resources were not universally accessible for all groups of people and the government benefit schemes would not have been able to cover the population equally at that time. The success story of the Thai UHC (Pannarunothai & Mills, 1997; Tangcharoensathien et al., 2014, 2015) is the main focal mechanism for developing other health-related policies, including the public long-term health care which focuses on community-based care.

Current national long-term care policy

In 2012, the National Health Security Committee and National Gerontology Committee certified a strategy for developing a LTC system at a national as well as a subdistrict level. The goal of the LTC policy was to include all Thai elderly. As a result, the elderly would be screened and cared for according to the level of their LTC needs with sustainable financial mechanisms. Services were to be provided on a community level through respite care, community LTC centres, and home care. An additional budget of about US$18 million (based on a cost study into community-based LTC in Lamsonthi subdistrict in 2014 by Wongsin et al. [2014]) was allocated to the NHSO to care for 100,000 dependent elderly in 1,000 subdistricts, including Bangkok. The benefits package included public health services such as screening, home care, health prevention and promotion, physical therapy, and social care services including daily living support (National Health Security Office, 2016).

By 2016, there was public awareness of Thailand facing an ageing society, and the Thai government was focusing on caring for the homebound and bedbound elderly, aiming to prevent the independent elderly from becoming ill and dependent. The NHSO also developed 6 strategies for implementing Thailand's LTC system. Each strategy is to focus on:

- establishing an accurate number of dependent elderly by each dependency level, such as homebound and bedbound, or with or without cognitive malfunction
- integrating LTC services in the community within the well-established primary healthcare system in each community
- developing a financial mechanism for a community-based LTC system
- developing human resources to meet the needs of LTC services in the community
- monitoring and assessing the services through LTC knowledge management and its related data and information
- reinforcing stakeholders' awareness and engagement with the LTC system through the legal support framework.

Each individual care plan is assessed on several levels. The current LTC benefit package is delivered according to the level of physical and cognitive ability of the dependent elderly (National Health Security Office, 2019).

Long-term care under the public health system

Currently, there are three main health insurance schemes in Thailand: the Social Security Scheme (SSS), the Civil Servant Medical Benefit Scheme (CSMBS), and the UHC scheme. The SSS covers formal workers and it has so-called tripartite funding methods comprised of the employee, the employer, and the government. This is the only public health insurance scheme where the beneficiary has to co-contribute. The CSMBS is health insurance for civil servants and their families. It is a tax-based funding system in which the Comptroller General's Department acts as the payer. The UHC is responsible for the population not covered by SSS and CSMBS. It is a tax-funded system and the NHSO acts as the purchaser.

With these three schemes, the main payment methods for hospital health services differ. The UHC is based on a capitation payment for outpatient services, and a Diagnosis-Related Groups

(DRGs) payment system for inpatient services. All elderly, except retired civil servants, are covered by the UHC. The elderly living in the community can access primary healthcare units and outpatient units, and the NHSO covers provider costs, e.g., hospitals through a capitation payment. When an elderly patient is admitted to an inpatient unit, the NHSO is the main purchaser with DRGs according to a fee schedule with a global budget payment. The SSS has a capitation payment for outpatient services and both capitation and DRGs payment for inpatient services. Capitation payment is also used for inpatient services when cases are rated as two or below for Adjusted Relative Weight (AdjRW). The SSS covers capitation payment for outpatient services and uses DRGs payment for inpatients with AdjRW higher than two (International Labour Organization, 2016). The CSMBS uses the DRGs system for inpatient services and fee-for-services for outpatient services.

When an elderly patient suffers from NCDs, has a homebound or bedbound condition, and receives health services in a hospital, the patient's health insurance will determine coverage of the provider's fees. Thus, the health care provided in a hospital must be financed under the acute care payment based on the system of each main purchaser.

The long-term care benefits package under the National Health Security Office

As the NHSO is the organisation that manages the health promotion and disease prevention budget for all Thai citizens, the UHC is the basis for the community-based LTC system in Thailand, providing health and social care services to eligible persons regardless of their specific public health coverage schemes. All eligible persons are entitled to accessing services in the community-based LTC system under the management of the NHSO.

Under the NHSO LTC system, a dependent elderly is a person with a score below 12 on the Barthel index of activities of daily living (Suriyanrattakorn & Chang, 2021). The LTC benefit is provided to all Thai-dependent older persons under any main health benefit scheme. An eligible person receives LTC services at home, or in a primary healthcare setting in their community, or at their community centre. Community-based LTC in Thailand aims to involve collaboration from all related stakeholders. In 2021, a budget of 26.93 million US$ was allocated for community-based LTC payments for the dependent elderly in every main health benefit scheme (National Health Security Office, 2020).

The benefit package under the LTC system is provided to the eligible elderly by dependency level. The NHSO, as the main responsible unit at a macro-level, has categorised the benefit packages into four types. These are provided through the community-based LTC in Thailand. Each dependency category for each dependent elderly is divided into four groups. The assessment of dependency groups for LTC benefit packages is conducted annually. The first group of benefit packages is for the elderly who somewhat move independently but who also need some domestic assistance for some daily living activities, such as eating and accessing the bathroom. The care plan for this first group is renewed at least every six months. The second group is for the persons who are part of the first group but with reduced cognitive functions. The third group is for those who cannot perform their daily living activities (bedbound) or who suffer from severe illness. The care plans for the second and third groups should be renewed at least every three months. The fourth group is for the elderly who are bedbound at an end-of-life stage and the care plan is updated on a monthly basis.

Table 4.2 Benefits package of community-based long-term care under the National Health Security System

Target group/ service package	The minimum frequency of community-based long-term care services provided in the package			Lump-sum cover (US$ per capita)
	Health services (at least...)	Home or community care (at least...)	Care-plan updated (at least...)	
The first group	Once a month	Once a month	Once a half-year	Not over 120
The second group	Once a month	Once a week	Once a quarter	90–180
The third group	Once a month	Once a week	Once a quarter	120–240
The fourth group	Twice a month	Twice a week	Once a month	150–300

Source: Long-term care for dependent elderly in the National Health Security System: National Health Security Office, 2019 (https://eng.National Health Security Office. go.th/assets/portals/1/files/Long-Term%20Care%20for%20Dependent%20Elderly_ Book.pdf).

Both health and social services are included in the community-based LTC packages. Health services are provided by health professionals from the hospital. Nurses provide nursing services and caregiver training for nursing-related care. Physical therapists provide rehabilitation services and psychologists, counsellors or clinical psychologists provide counselling services. Nutrition and pharmaceutical assistance, for example, could also be part of the health services that older persons need. Trained caregivers provide home or community care, including basic nursing and housing keeping. In assisting with movement or other physical functions, the local administrative organisation (LAO) may act as the clinical devices and equipment distributor to the elderly based on the person's needs and the health professional's recommendation. The care manager provides an individual care plan for each elderly in a timely fashion. Table 4.2 illustrates the frequency and coverage of services.

Stakeholder involvement in the public long-term care system and its financing

There are many government sectors involved in the development of the LTC system in Thailand. The MoPH has developed a system of LTC for the dependent elderly. There are some areas considered to be LTC best-practice and some of those are pilot programs, such as in Lopburi, Chiang Mai, Khon Kaen, and Ubon Ratchathani (A. P. S. Sasat; Tantuvanit; Wongsin et al., 2014). The MoPH also set the standard for LTC and its assessment. The NHSO is the main purchaser of community-based LTC in Thailand. The results from this main purchaser method drive the outcomes of the LTC services such as health promotion and prevention, essential treatments, medical rehabilitation, palliative care in the community, and contributing to the subdistrict funds. The Ministry of Social Development and Human Security (MSDHS) is the main government department for social and welfare services. The MSDHS supports LTC through the mechanism of the National Committee for the Elderly. The MSDHS also provides public welfare to the elderly such as public shelters, training for social assistant volunteers, and day-care services in the centre for the development of the elderly's quality of life, and it administers the budget allocated for implementing the friendly environment to the dependent elderly. The LAO under the Ministry of Interior is responsible for allocating the monthly senior subsistence allowance and supporting the services provided by the VHV.

In terms of budget allocation, the NHSO divides its budget for the public community LTC into two sections. One section of the budget allocation covers primary care health facilities such as the contracting unit for primary care (CUP) and the primary care unit (PCU). The NHSO employs a lump sum payment for this section, which accounts for about US$3,191 per primary healthcare facility unit per year in 2019 (National Health Security Office, 2019). This part of the budget covers the screening process of the elderly, the care plan construction, some service delivery, and technical assistance to the LAO. The other part of the budget funds the LTC capitation by headcount, which is US$191.5 per person per year, to the local health security fund managed by the LAO (National Health Security Office, 2019). This part of the budget covers LTC services by the proposed care plan and also the community caregiver costs.

LTC policy tends to focus on public community-based LTC with the budget allocated through UHC by the NHSO. The NHSO is responsible for allocating the capitation for all eligible persons in each community, and any Thai citizen aged 60 and over with dependent conditions is eligible. Community providers such as health professionals in PCUs or VHV screen the level of dependency using cognitive screening through the Barthel activities of the daily living instrument. A person who is deemed dependent is eligible for public community LTC services. In 2019, the NHSO received a budget of about US$29 million to cover LTC services for 152,800 eligible persons (National Health Security Office, 2019) (Figure 4.4).

Thailand has also continued to improve the social welfare for its ageing population. According to law, a compulsory 2% surcharge on the price of unhealthy products such as tobacco, sugar, or alcohol, a so-called sin-tax, has to be used for health promotion services via the Thai Health Promotion Foundation (Javadinasab et al., 2020).

Some government agencies were allocated a budget for aged care in which some activities are related to the target group of the LTC system. Table 4.3 shows the government's budget allocation to the public agencies in Thailand (Department of Local Administration of the Ministry of Interior, 2020, 2021; Government of Thailand, 2021; National Health Security Office, 2021). The LAO is often being chosen as the main department for managing allocations from the agencies as it has the closest relationship with the population. It has been found that the LAO and NHSO were allocated the largest budget amounts (National Health Security Office, 2021). Table 4.3 also reflects the social benefit dimension for supporting the elderly in

Lump-sum for the Contracted Unit of Primary Care

Service unit	LAO (Fund)	Capitation	NHSO

| Care Plan | The dependent elderly in the community | | *Supported Sectors by its duties |

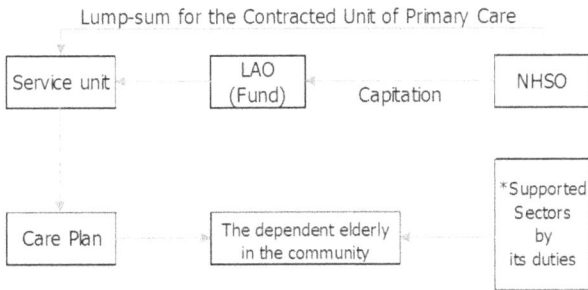

* The supported Sectors such as Ministry of Interior, Ministry of Social Development and Human Security, Thai Health Promotion Foundation, The National Health Commission office, Health Systems Research Institute, and private sectors

Figure 4.4 Pathway of budget allocation for community-based long-term care under the National Health Security System

Source: Long-term care for dependent elderly in the National Health Security System, National Health Security Office (2019).

Thailand. There are many projects that the government is attempting to implement to support the ageing population, especially dependent persons.

In terms of the monthly senior subsistence allowance, the age group 60–69 receives a monthly allowance of US$22.49; the population aged 70–79 allowance of US$25.70; the population aged 80–89 allowance of US$28.92, and the population aged 90 and over receives a monthly allowance of US$35.34, respectively (Office of the Secretariat of the House of Representatives, 2019). Despite Thailand's attempt to implement and improve the budget allocation to its ageing population, inequity persists among different groups of the elderly due to different pension benefits. The elderly who receive the monthly civil servant pension are in a better financial position than the elderly who receive the monthly senior subsistence allowance. In 2019, the budget for about 700,000 former civil servants was US$7.19 million, while the budget for the 9 million elderly receiving the senior subsistence allowance was US$2,310.50 million (Rakbumnet, 2019).

In 2017, the Survey of Older Persons found that 92% of the elderly in Thailand were satisfied or very satisfied with the benefits they received from the government (see Table 4.4).

Table 4.3 Budget funding from the government agencies for long-term care in Thailand, 2021–2022

Budget allocation related to aging population	Budget funding (US$)	Responsible agency
*Monthly senior subsistence allowance *in Fiscal Year 2021*	492,777,416.77	The Local Administrative Organisation
*Monthly disabled subsistence allowance *in Fiscal Year 2021*	86,835,232.88	The Local Administrative Organisation
**Budget for health services for dependent persons living in the communities *in Fiscal Year 2022*	29,762,468.26	National Health Security Office
***Volunteer remuneration *from July 2020 to September 2021*	28,042,204.88	Department of Local Administration, Ministry of Interior
****National Strategy Creating Social Security *in Fiscal Year 2022*	9,450,275.35	Department of Older Persons, Ministry of Social Development and Human Security
****Ageing society preparedness integration plans *in Fiscal Year 2022*	6,719,316.65	Department of Older Persons, Ministry of Social Development and Human Security
**Training Volunteers for the dependent elderly *from July 2020 to September 2021*	4,440,015.77	Department of Local Administration, Ministry of Interior
****Ageing society preparedness integration plans *in Fiscal Year 2022**	2,989,494.19	Mahidol University, Ministry of Higher Education, Science, Research and Innovation
****Ageing society preparedness integration plans *in Fiscal Year 2022**	1,953,888.30	National Science and Technology Development Agency, Ministry of Higher Education, Science, Research and Innovation
****Older fund *in Fiscal Year 2022**	1,893,768.66	Ministry of Social Development and Human Security
****Ageing society preparedness integration plans *in Fiscal Year 2022**	1,776,382.06	Department of Health, Ministry of Public Health
****Ageing society preparedness integration plans *in Fiscal Year 2022**	1,232,452.62	Digital Economy Promotion Agency

****Ageing society preparedness integration plans *in Fiscal Year 2022*	1,149,277.10	Thailand Centre of Excellence for Life Sciences (Public Organisation)
****National Strategy Creating opportunities and social equality *in Fiscal Year 2022*	702,017.04	Department of Older Persons, Ministry of Social Development and Human Security
****Ageing society preparedness integration plans *in Fiscal Year 2022*	601,196.40	Department of Skill Development, Ministry of Labor
****Ageing society preparedness integration plans *in Fiscal Year 2022*	501,818.64	Office of the Permanent Secretary Ministry of Public Health

Source:
*Budget allocation for senior's subsistence allowance and disabled's subsistence of Financial Year 2021, Department of Local Government Promotion, Ministry of Interior, 2020.
**Criteria for managing National Health Security Budget of Financial Year 2022; National Health Security Office, 2021.
***Annual Report 2020, Department of Local Administration of the Ministry of Interior, 2021.
****Budget for the Financial 2022Year, Government of Thailand, 2021.
Note.1 Thai Baht equals US$0.30 as of 2 November 2021. Fiscal Year 2021 covered 1st October 2020 to 30th September 2021. Fiscal Year 2022 covers 1st October 2021 to 30th September 2022.

Table 4.4 Number and proportion of the elderly's satisfaction with the public benefit systems in Thailand

The public benefit	Healthcare services	%	Subsistence allowance	%	Subsistence allowance for disabled	%
Very unsatisfied	67,600	0.72	77,576	0.83	54,809	0.59
Unsatisfied	362,179	3.87	811,344	8.66	99,826	1.07
Satisfied	7,374,356	78.73	5,735,054	61.23	791,325	8.45
Very satisfied	1,242,693	13.27	1,797,567	19.19	264,756	2.83
Never access to service	319,338	3.41	944,626	10.09	8,155,450	87.07
Total	9,366,166	100	9,366,167	100	9,366,166	100

Source: National Statistical Office of Thailand, Survey of Older Persons (2017).

Community-based long-term care in practice

*The oversight role of National Health
Security Office (*NHSO*)*

The NHSO is the main purchaser of community-based LTC supporting
the dependent elderly. The NHSO manages the budget allocation of
both the primary healthcare facilities and the LAOs. Based on the
NHSO Board regulations, the capitation was about US$192.78 per
dependent elderly per year in 2021.

The NHSO has developed the so-called LTC program which is a
software program used by the service providers, the LAOs, and the
NHSO. This program is used for recording information on the benefit
package, payment information, and the outcomes of the services. At
the meso- and micro-level, the LAO and service providers can inspect
and manage the care plan through the program. At the macro-level,
the NHSO can monitor and evaluate the LTC services and the system
in a specific area or at a national level.

To implement the LTC services for the eligible elderly in a particular
community, the service providers in the primary healthcare setting,
such as The Tambon Health Promoting Hospitals (THPH), use the
activities of daily living instrument to determine whether a person
is home-bound or bed-bound. Once the dependent elderly have been
identified, the service providers record the data into the LTC program
provided by the NHSO. Each LAO subsequently analyses the recorded
cases as the LAO is the department that is closest to its population
and is familiar with the people in their community. This allows them
to verify the accuracy of the identified cases. After this verification,
the service provider must develop a care plan with the approval of the
LAO. In addition to the LAO's verification, the NHSO assesses the
identified cases and the proposed care plan that the service provider
has recorded in the LTC program. The NHSO provides the prospective
budget allocation in two ways. First, the NHSO provides a lump-sum
payment of US$3,191 to a specific service facility. Second, the NHSO
provides the capitation payment of US$191.5 per capita to the LAO
through the Local Health Security Fund. Care managers and caregivers are responsible for delivering the LTC services in the community,
as proposed in the care plan. Once LTC services have been provided
for nine months, the service providers conduct activities of daily living assessment to measure the dependency outcome. The results are
subsequently recorded in the LTC program in order for the additional
budget for LTC services to continue. After providing LTC services for

one year, the care providers again report on the outcome to the NHSO board.

After implementing the LTC policy in 2013, the family care team and care manager are considered part of the public community-based LTC system. The NHSO proposed a ratio in relation to the number of caregivers, care managers, and dependent elderly where one care manager should be responsible for five caregivers and 35–40 dependent older persons, meaning that one caregiver would be responsible for about four dependent older persons. The number of responsible dependent elderly may, however, vary subject to the level of physical and cognitive function of the person.

The role of primary health care as public long-term healthcare providers

Focusing on community-based care, the primary healthcare system is equipped for providing services with the infrastructure already in place in every subdistrict in Thailand. The Health Promoting Hospitals located in every subdistrict are responsible for the residents living in their particular subdistrict.

The primary healthcare system in Thailand provides six types of service (The Committee of Primary Health Care System, 2020), for example, advisory committee, health advisory services, and health services appointments; referral services and continuing of care services; health-promotion and health literacy for the person, their family and the community as a whole.

The providers in the primary healthcare system include both formal and informal providers. The formal providers are the health professionals providing the services in the Tambon Health Promotion Hospitals (the primary healthcare unit in a subdistrict) and home care. In 2021 (Ministry of Public Health, 2021), there were 10,876 primary healthcare units with 62,628 full-time health professionals. Considering these primary healthcare units, 9,142 units provided LTC home-visit services in the patient's household. The health professionals include, for example, general practitioners (generally based in a community hospital), pharmacists (generally based in a community hospital), nurses, public health technical officers, and physical therapists.

One of Thailand's success stories is the VHV, who represent the informal providers. In 2020, there were 1,027,036 VHVs in rural and urban areas in Thailand (Foundation of Thai Gerontology Research and Development Institute, 2021). The ratio of VHV per household was 1:10–15 depending on the number of VHV in the particular area

(Chachoengsao Provincial Health Office, 2017). A VHV is a registered village layperson (over 1 million nationwide) and their role is to support the primary healthcare services focusing on health promotion and prevention activities. They might work as the VHV at the primary healthcare setting or in a person's home. Once the LTC policy has been implemented, their work might include LTC services as well as activities of daily living/instrumental activities of daily living services. Some of the VHV have been trained as community caregivers. In 2021, there were 69,767 caregivers who provided activities of daily living/instrumental activities of daily living support to the dependent elderly under the community-based LTC system (Ministry of Public Health, 2021).

Case study 1: Lamsonthi District—pioneer of the community-based long-term care system in Thailand (Since 2006)

Lamsonthi is a district located in the Lopburi province in central Thailand. This is a rural and remote area where most of the population lives below the poverty line. However, Lamsonthi has been a successful pioneer of the community-based LTC system in Thailand. The pilot began without any policy directions from the central government or the MoPH. Lamsonthi developed their integrated community health system focusing on primary healthcare management using a patient-centred approach and is managed by a multidisciplinary team. They designed the "Team and Integration of Health and Social Care Sector" as a concept for the LTC system for this area. Based on this concept, the Lamsonthi district's LTC committee worked as a care coordinator to provide a care policy to each subdistrict operating unit and provider at each household unit. The health and social sectors worked together from policy design to management and delivery of services. There were two lines of support for the patients in the community: the Tambon Health Promotion Hospitals and the Lamsonthi District Hospital. The results from this pilot strengthened the primary healthcare system. There was a registered nurse practice in each of the six THPHs. Other services included primary healthcare services and treatments such as rehabilitation from physical therapist, counselling and assessment from a clinical psychologist, and meals from a nutritionist. Professional consultants also offered telemedicine. The health professionals aimed to integrate the health services with social welfare to improve the quality of life of the dependent persons in their community. The care team for the dependent persons was based in the hospitals but the services were provided in the patients' homes. The health professionals also provided basic training to the VHV and family caregivers. A digital database was developed to record the patients' data. Other health staff members were included in the care team to provide comprehensive LTC services such as improving the patients' environment and adjusting orthoses and prostheses. After 2011, it was determined that for the LTC system to be effective, there was a need for greater collaboration between the healthcare team and the LAO. A LTC centre was established, and the care was divided into three levels: district level, subdistrict level, and household level. The LTC district committee was established to achieve collaboration between the LAOs and the health facilities in the Lamsonthi district. Their active community-based LTC team included three registered nurses, three physical therapists, two psychologists, one occupational therapist, one nutritionist, one carpenter, and three drivers.

Case study 2: A prototype of comprehensive dementia care under the community-based long-term care system (Since 2018)

Persons with dementia need LTC services even if they are not suffering from a reduced physical functional status. In 2020, dementia cases in the elderly population represented 1% of the total population. However, it is estimated that about 2.1%, or over a million people in Thailand, will suffer from dementia in 2040. The coordination of the comprehensive dementia care network comprises the Ministry of Public Health, the Alzheimer's and Related Disorders Association of Thailand, the Faculty of Medicine Ramathibodi Hospital-Mahidol University, the Foundation of Thai Gerontology Research and Development Institute, the Thai Nurses Society for people with Dementia, and the Network

(*Conitnued*)

of Operational Area Level and Service Settings Association. Pilot projects were launched in four areas—Ban Fang District; Khon Khan Province, Muang District; Nakhon Ratchasima Province, Lamsonthi District; Lopburi Province, Kirirat Nikhom District; and Surat Thani Province. The prototype areas were developed by the community dementia care network system. The process begins with a screening system by the LTC team in the hospital and in the patient's household. The Ministry of Public Health is planning to expand the prototype of comprehensive dementia care under the community-based LTC system to all 13 health regions throughout the country. It is suggested that the LAOs should act as support units for this LTC system, especially the social supports (Chuakhamfoo et al., 2020), such as providing vehicles for the referral system, searching the elderly at risk of dementia in the community, and providing a safety system to prevent the elderly from getting lost (Foundation of Thai Gerontology Research and Development Institute, 2021).

Roles of the local governments

In 2020, the primary healthcare units provided health services to 72,878 villages covering 13,982,372 households. Approximately 6,722 subdistricts of a total of 7,255 subdistricts (or 92%) operated community-based LTC systems in 2020 (Foundation of Thai Gerontology Research and Development Institute, 2021). Most LAOs are Subdistrict Administrative Organisations with supportive roles in the LTC system in their respective community. They operate the Subdistrict Health Fund which subsidises the THPH. The Subdistrict Administrative Organisations support the long-term social care in their communities by providing compensation to the Elderly Care Volunteers (ECVs; volunteers trained by the Ministry of Social Development and the Human Security) living in 1,589 subdistricts throughout the country. The role of the ECVs is to provide home visits and care advice to the dependent elderly and their caregivers The Subdistrict Administrative Organisations also provide subsidies to the Senior Citizen Center in their community (Foundation of Thai Gerontology Research and Development Institute, 2021; Ministry of Public Health, 2021; Suwanrada et al., 2014).

According to the legal framework (Ratchakitcha, 2018), the local governments can manage their provision and co-funding to support the community-based LTC system. The local governments, such as the municipality, the Subdistrict Administrative Organisation, the Pattaya City Self Administrating Municipality, and the Bangkok Metropolitan Administration, are responsible for allocating human resources relating to the community-based LTC for the dependent elderly in their area. The Provincial Administrative Organisations are responsible for the training of the LTC human resources.

In terms of co-funding, the local government allocates the budget relating to the community-based LTC for the dependent elderly of its responsible area. Generally, the LAO allocates the budget for human resource development such as training and compensation for the service providers.

Human resources for public long-term care in Thailand

In terms of long-term health care, human resources should come from the formal healthcare sector to ensure patients receive quality care and quality services. The care manager is the main health professional involved in the community-based LTC system. They are a qualified medical doctor, nurse, or public health personnel. The Department of Health, which falls under the Ministry of Public Health, is responsible for the training of the care managers, who also have experience in aged care. The role of the care manager is to review the services provided to the dependent elderly. Thus, they must have expertise in clinical services to create an appropriate care plan for each dependent elderly according to their LTC needs. The care manager is also the contact person for the coordination of clinical services and non-medical services. The care manager is also the person who chooses the caregiver and they are the key person who assigns, assesses, and coordinates the implementation of the service with the multi-disciplinary team.

Long-term social care personnel

The long-term social care personnel provide the non-medical care as part of the LTC services. There are both formal and informal personnel in community long-term social care. To qualify as a care manager, they need to complete at least 70 hours of care manager training.

A formal caregiver is a non-professional person who is trained as a caregiver by achieving 70 (Intermediate level) or 420 (Advanced level) hours of training by the Department of Health, Ministry of Public Health. The caregiver might come from the VHV and is interested in being a caregiver in the community-based LTC system. The main roles of the caregiver involve assisting the dependent elderly with particular activities of daily living, including meal preparation and assist with self-care. The caregiver is providing their services under the supervision of the care manager. The training includes knowledge of aged care and services provided to the elderly such as basic assistance in health care, drug use, first aid, and nutrition (Bureau of Elderly Health Department of Health Ministry of Public Health, 2014a). Moreover, caregivers also ensure the home environment is safe and assist the elderly in case of an emergency. The training also includes knowledge of aged care from both a health and social aspect, interpersonal skills (e.g., interview, assessment, and ethics), resource management, and legal issues relating to aged care management (Bureau of Elderly Health Department of Health Ministry of Public Health, 2014b).

An ECV is a non-professional person who has completed 120 hours of training by any department in the Ministry of Public Health or another ministry such as the Department of Local Administration, Ministry of Interior. Training covers the content of basic elderly assistance, interpersonal relationship skills, the roles of local government, and case records and referrals. Upon completing their training, they are able to provide basic and essential care to the dependent elderly. The benefits of having a trained ECV in the household include knowledge sharing with other family members and improving the coordination of the elderly's household and the VHV. In 2020, there were about 24,293 ECVs in Thailand (Foundation of Thai Gerontology Research and Development Institute, 2021).

Non-government organisations involved in the long-term care system

In terms of LTC research and capacity building, there are other key agencies involved in the improvement of the LTC system in Thailand. The councils of public health professionals have crucial roles in training and developing the standards of community-based LTC services. The Foundation of Thai Gerontology Research and Development Institute (TGRI) and other research agencies are the knowledge hub for improving the LTC system, including policy directions, management in different context areas, and suggested treatment or best-practice.

In terms of social services, Lloyd-Sherlock et al. (2021) investigated the residential LTC services in Bangkok and found that some NGOs in Thailand provide LTC facilities which can care for about 450 people. The elderly usually live in the provided LTC facility until they pass away. Some religious organisations such as Buddhist temples provide shelters for vulnerable elderly and some work with community health providers (Lloyd-Sherlock, 2021).

Sasat et al. studied the LTC institutions in Thailand and found that in 2013, there were a limited number of aged care institutes which classify as LTC institutes in Thailand (Sasat et al., 2013). The institutional care approach is not popular in Thailand as the cost is perceived as higher than home-based or community-based care. However, institutional care needs to be part of the LTC system in Thailand in order to respond to the demand of the urban areas, or to serve as respite care, or a place of living for those with no family caregivers. To relieve the burden on the public health system, private organisations or NGOs need to be part of the LTC system. However, the administrative roles of public and private organisations and quality controls must be clear and of an acceptable standard. Social care as part of many LTC activities may have its activities divided into formal or informal categories to determine type of care and providers.

Discussion and potential directions for long-term care in Thailand

Issues relating to community-based long-term care

The advantages of a community-based LTC pathway include improving the equity among the dependent elderly who require care, especially the persons who live in their home. Since the implementation of the system, the number of LAOs participating in this LTC system has been increasing over time. The close monitoring from both the LAOs and NHSO is a positive start to an integrated system of the social and health sectors that can improve the LTC system in Thailand.

However, the current community-based system relies on the government budget only. There is currently no plan for implementing a co-payment from the Thai population. The main budget considerations include basic coverage and cost-effectiveness issues. Services provided to the elderly may differ across the country, as they may depend on the context of each community, including a varying demand for LTC services and the availability of LTC in each area. There needs to be standard pricing and payment for community-based LTC. Some studies attempted to analyse the cost of intermediate care and LTC from a value-based aspect. The studies employed the DRG codes and Rehabilitation impairment categories for analysing the cost by group. The results suggest that payment for acute care in Thailand is not a suitable basis of payment for LTC (Pannarunothai et al., 2021a, 2021b).

In addition, the quality assurance of community-based LTC in Thailand is still in its planning stage. Current progress reports of the program need to include factors such as quality of life of the elderly and their family caregivers as the outcome of the dependency level might not be sufficient to provide effective information on the quality of the services.

The future direction of long-term care in Thailand

As mentioned earlier in the chapter, the directions for the LTC system tend to come from the public system. However, the system acts reactively rather than proactively. The system depends on resource allocation being determined by government policy. Moreover, there is insufficient capacity to provide adequate services to the dependent elderly. At times, public providers still hold a "charity mentality". Thus, the system is in part fragmented, especially in terms of social care. Proactive LTC planning and implementation need to be established to resolve these issues of inadequate services and fragmented care.

As most rural areas in Thailand still rely on the eastern-world norm where a family member is the main caregiver for the dependent elderly, the quality of care by unpaid family caregivers is a point of concern for the community-based/home-based LTC system (Chuakhamfoo & Pannarunothai, 2014). Even though the Ministry of Public Health has established a Family Care Team (multidisciplinary team) to provide care, there have been a number of older persons who have suffered from comorbidities or relapse. This is one of the main causes for revisits or readmission in which there is a need for specialist treatment and longer episodes of care. Thus, the quality of care by the caregiver is crucial in alleviating the situation.

Access to and provision of long-term healthcare services are other challenges. The decentralisation of services in Thailand caused various issues over a few decades due to political policies. This affected the support mechanisms for the elderly, their families, and their communities. For policy planning, there is a need to clarify the roles and actions of the actors at each level of community-based LTC, including at a micro-, meso-, and macro-level. At a micro-level, the planning policy should reflect the support system for the family care team, and the social care mechanisms need to be supported by a trained care worker in the community, who collaborates with their LAO. At a meso-level, the planning policy should provide a concrete picture of the care manager's responsibility, such as care coordination. At a macro-level, the central government should address the support systems for the LTC policy such as standard guidelines, a national training hub, license controls, standard pricing, and legal support.

Sustainability of long-term care in Thailand

When Thailand decided that its LTC system should be shifted from the hospital to the community or household, the supporting financial system was still based on acute care procedures. The financial mechanism for post-acute care or non-acute care is still in development. Ideally, the payment mechanism should shift from fee-for-service to value-based payment as it is expected that the latter payment model results in better service outcomes. In practice, to employ a value-based payment to all public healthcare schemes still raises questions, such as what results should be expected from LTC services, and whether the health conditions or dependency level is acceptable or worsening. Finally, Thailand's economic security is an issue of concern as it is a middle-income country with an ageing population of more than 20%. Preparing the working age to be part of a healthy ageing population, with a healthy personal financial wellbeing for their retirement should be a parallel policy action to relieve the burden for the future LTC system. Policymakers and public–private partnerships should aim to be more proactive (Zwi, 2021). Thailand needs to shift its LTC issue from being a burden of the health and social care system to be an income source. Strengthening the systems through an integrated approach will encourage involvement by stakeholders. Engaging all stakeholders in managing the LTC system can prevent the fragmentation of services and instead offer a system of seamless care. However, the human resource issue needs to be planned and prepared for to ensure sufficient and adequate service provisions.

References

Asian Development Bank. (2020). Country diagnostic study on long-term care in Thailand. Manila. Retrieved from https://www.adb.org/publications/thailand-country-diagnostic-study-long-term-care

Buracom, P. (2011). The determinants and distributional effects of public education, health, and welfare spending in Thailand. *Asian Affairs: An American Review, 38*(3), 113–142.

Bureau of Elderly Health Department of Health Ministry of Public Health. (2014a). *Elderly Care Giver Training Program 420 Hrs.*Nonthaburi: Bureau of Elderly Health Department of Health Ministry of Public Health.

Bureau of Elderly Health Department of Health Ministry of Public Health. (2014b). *Elderly Care Manager Training Program 70 Hrs: The Second Batch.* Nonthaburi: Bureau of Elderly Health Department of Health Ministry of Public Health. Retrieved from https://hpc13.anamai.moph.go.th/ewt_news.php?nid=69&filename=15

Chachoengsao Provincial Health Office. (2017). *Standard Operating Procedure.* Chachoengsao: Retrieved from http://www.oic.go.th/FILEWEB/CABINFO-CENTER4/DRAWER076/GENERAL/DATA0000/00000081.PDF

Chuakhamfoo, N., & Pannarunothai, S. (2014). Long-term care: What Thailand needs? *BMC Public Health, 14*(Suppl 1), P6.

Chuakhamfoo, N., Phanthunane, P., Chansirikarn, S., & Pannarunothai, S. (2020). Health and long-term care of the elderly with dementia in rural Thailand. *BMJ Open, 10*(3), e032637.

Department of Local Administration of the Ministry of Interior. (2020). *Budget Allocation for Senior's Subsistence Allowance and Disabled's Subsistence of Financial Year 2021.* Bangkok. Retrieved from http://www.dla.go.th/upload/document/type2/2020/12/24591_1_1606978521875.pdf.

Department of Local Administration of the Ministry of Interior. (2021). *Annual Report 2020.* Bangkok. Retrieved from http://www.dla.go.th/upload/ebook/column/2021/3/2310_6190.pdf

Economic Research Institute for ASEAN and East Asia. (2019). Demand of long-term care: Care need. In H. Reiko (Ed.), *Demand and Supply of Long-Term Care for Older Persons in Asia* (pp. 6–9). Jakarta: Economic Research Institute for ASEAN and East Asia. Retrieved from https://www.eria.org/uploads/media/7_RPR_FY2018_08_Chapter_2.pdf

Foundation of Thai Gerontology Research and Development Institute. (2021). *Situation of the Thai Older Persons 2020.* Nakhon Pathom: Institute for Population and Social Research, Mahidol University.Retrieved from https://www.dop.go.th/download/knowledge/th1635826412-975_0.pdf.

Government of Thailand. (2021). Budget for Financial Year 2022. Retrieved from http://www.ratchakitcha.soc.go.th/DATA/PDF/2564/A/062/T_0001.PDF.

Goldstein, S. (1971). Urbanization in Thailand, 1947–1967. *Demography, 8*(2), 205–223.

Institute for Population and Social Research of Mahidol University. (2021). *Survey of COVID-19 Lockdown Policy Effects to Low-Income Older Persons in Thailand.* Nakhon Pathom: Institute for Population and Social Research, Mahidol University.

Institute for Population and Social Research of Mahidol University. (2022, 1st January 2022). Thailandometers. *Current Thai Population.* Nakhon Pathom. Retrieved from http://www.thailandometers.mahidol.ac.th/index.php?#population

International Labour Organization. (2016). *Actuarial Valuation of Thailand Social Security Scheme Administered by the Social Security Office as of 31 December 2013 Report to the Government: Thailand.* Retrieved from https://www.social-protection.org/gimi/gess/RessourcePDF.action?ressource.ressourceId=53893

Javadinasab, H., Masoudi Asl, I., Vosoogh-Moghaddam, A , & Najafi, B. (2020). Comparing selected countries using sin tax policy in sustainable health financing: Implications for developing countries. *The International Journal of Health Planning and Management, 35*(1), 68–78.

Jitapunkul, S., & Chayovan, N. (2001). National policies on ageing in Thailand. Retrieved from http://extranet.who.int/countryplanningcycles/sites/default/files/planning_cycle_repository/thailand/national_policies_on_ageing_in_thailand_2001_-_2020.pdf.

Jitapunkul, S., & Wivatvanit, S. (2008). National policies and programs for the aging population in Thailand. *Ageing International, 33*(1), 62–74.

Kaufman, N. D., Chasombat, S., Tanomsingh, S., Rajataramya, B., & Potempa, K. (2011). Public health in Thailand: Emerging focus on noncommunicable diseases. *The International Journal of Health Planning and Management, 26*(3), e197–e212.

Lee, E. K. (2012). *A Study on Patterns of Attitude and Behavior toward Parental Support: Comparing South Korea, Japan, Taiwan and Thailand in the Mid-2000s* (Doctoral dissertation, 서울대학교 대학원).

Lloyd-Sherlock, P. G., Sasat, S., Sanee, A., Miyoshi, Y., & Lee, S. (2021). The rapid expansion of residential long-term care services in Bangkok: A challenge for regulation. *Journal of Public Health and Development, 19*(2), 89–101.

Ministry of Public Health. (2021). Data of health resources: Primary health care units. Nonthaburi. Retrieved from http://gishealth.moph.go.th/pcu/admin/report.php

Monkhlung, R., Phosing, P., & Kenaphoom, S. (2016). Factors affecting achievement policy implementation of elderly's health service in the local administrative organization. *Prae-wa Kalasin Journal of Kalasin University, 3*(2), 133–153.

Moroz, H., Naddeo, J., Ariyapruchya, K., Walker, T., Yang, J., Glinskaya, E., Jain, H., Lamanna, F., Laowong, P., Nair, A., Palacios, R., Tansanguanwong, P., & Viriyataveekul, S. (2021). *Aging and the labor market in Thailand.* Retrieved from https://openknowledge.worldbank.org/handle/10986/35691

National Health Security Office. (2016). *Handbook on Support for Management of Long-Term Health Care for Dependent Elderly under the National Health Security System.* Nonthaburi. Retrieved from https://www.chiangmaihealth.go.th/cmpho_web/document/200417158709406445.pdf

National Health Security Office. (2019). *Long-term care for dependent elderly in the National Health Security System.* Nonthaburi: National Health Security Office.

National Health Security Office. (2020). *Manual of National Health Security Fund: Financial Year 2021.* Nonthaburi. Retrieved from: https://www.nhso.go.th/storage/files/shares/PDF/fund_man01.pdf

National Health Security Office. (2021). *Criteria for Managing National Health Security Budget of Financial Year 2022.* Nonthaburi.

National Statistical Office of Thailand. (2002). *Thailand's Older Population: Social and Economic Support as Assessed in 2002.* Bangkok: National Statistical Office of Thailand.

National Statistical Office of Thailand. (2018). Survey of Older Persons. In National Statistical Office of Thailand (Ed.), *The number of Older Persons by the need for caregiver in helping with Activity of Daily Living, main caregiver, gender.* Bangkok: National Statistical Office of Thailand.

Office of the Secretariat of the House of Representatives. (2019). The Constitution of the Kingdom of Thailand with the elder welfares. In Office of the Secretariat of the House of Representatives (Ed.), (2019 ed.). Bangkok.

Office of the National Economic and Social Development Council. (2013). The estimation of the population in Thailand B.E. 2010–2040. Bangkok.

Organization for Economic Co-operation and Development. (2007). *Conceptual Framework and Methods for Analysis of Data Sources for Long-Term Care Expenditure.* Paris: OECD Publishing.

Pannarunothai, S., Khiaocharoen, O., Zungsontiporn, C., Riewpaiboon, A., Phantunane, P., Khotthong, K., & Chuakhamfoo, N. N. (2021a). *Standrad Costing and Payment for Intermediate Care in Thailand.* Nonthaburi: Division of Health Economics and Health Security, Ministry of Public Health of Thailand.

Pannarunothai, S., Khiaocharoen, O., Zungsontiporn, C., Riewpaiboon, A., Phantunane, P., Khotthong, K., & Chuakhamfoo, N. N. (2021b). *Standard Costing and Payment for Long-Term Care in Thailand.* Nonthaburi: Division of Health Economics and Health Security, Ministry of Public Health of Thailand.

Pannarunothai, S., & Mills, A. (1997). The poor pay more: health-related inequality in Thailand. *Social Science & Medicine, 44*(12), 1781–1790.

Prasitsiriphon, O., Jeger, F., Tharachompoo, A., & Sakunphanit, T. (2013). *Costing Model for Long-Term Care System in Thailand.* Nonthaburi: Health System Research Office.

Prasitsiriphon, O., Jeger, F., Tharachompoo, A., & Sakunphanit, T. (2014). *Costing Model for Long-Term Care System in Thailand (Revised Version).* Nonthaburi: Health System Research Office.

Rakbumnet, C. (2019). *Guidelines for Budget Management for Social Welfare in Aged-Care.* Secretariat of the House of Representatives. Bangkok. Retrieved from https://www.parliament.go.th/ewtadmin/ewt/parbudget/ewt_dl_link.php?nid=639

Ratchakitcha. (2018). *Responsibilities of the local government on dependent elderly care*: The Cabinet and the Government Gazette Printing.

Sasat, S. (2019). *Standard of Care for Long-term Care in Thailand.* Nonthaburi: Health Insurance System Research Office.

Sasat, S., Choowattanapakorn, T., Pukdeeprom, T., Lertrat, P., & Aroonsang, P. (2013). Long-term care institutions in Thailand. *Journal of Health Research, 27*(6), 413–418.

Sumriddetchkajorn, K., Shimazaki, K., Ono, T., Kusaba, T., Sato, K., & Kobayashi, N. (2019). Universal health coverage and primary care, Thailand. *Bulletin of the World Health Organization, 97*(6), 415.

Suriyanrattakorn, S., & Chang, C.-L. (2021). Long-term care (LTC) policy in Thailand on the homebound and bedridden elderly happiness. *Health Policy Open, 2*, 100026.

Suwanrada, W., Pothisiri, W., Prachuabmoh, V., Siriboon, S., Bangkaew, B., & Milintangul, C. (2014). *Community-Based Integrated Approach for Older Persons' Long-Term Care in Thailand.* Bangkok: College of Population Studies, Chulalongkorn University.

Tangcharoensathien, V., Limwattananon, S., Patcharanarumol, W., & Thammatacharee, J. (2014). Monitoring and evaluating progress towards universal health coverage in Thailand. *PLoS Medicine, 11*(9), e1001726.

Tangcharoensathien, V., Limwattananon, S., Patcharanarumol, W., Thammatacharee, J., Jongudomsuk, P., & Sirilak, S. (2015). Achieving universal health coverage goals in Thailand: The vital role of strategic purchasing. *Health Policy and Planning, 30*(9), 1152–1161.

Tantuvanit, N. (2021). Home-and Community-based Care: Household, Community, Local, and Network Long-term Care for Older People. In D. Lorthanavanich & O. Komazawa (Eds.), Population Ageing in Thailand Long-term care Model: Review of Population Aging Practices and Policies, ERIA Research Project Report FY2021 No. 06b (Vol. 2, pp. 21). Bangkok: Economic Research Institute for ASEAN and East Asia and Ageing Business & Care Development Centre (ABCD Centre) of Thammasat Business School of Thammasat University. Retrieved from https://www.eria.org/uploads/media/Research-Project-Report/2021-06/Vol-2_00-Long-term-Care-Model_Review-of-Population-Ageing-Practices-and-Policies.pdf#page=27.

The Asian Population and Development Association. (1995). *Report on the Survey of Urbanization and Development in Asian Countries: Thailand.* Retrieved from https://www.apda.jp/pdf/p03_kousei/1995_Thailand_E.pdf

The Committee of Primary Health Care System. (2020). *Primary Health Care Services the individuals shall be recieved B.E. 2563.*

UNESCO Institute for Statistics. (2021). *World Development Indicators.* Retrieved from: https://data.worldbank.org/indicator/SE.SEC.CUAT.UP.FE.ZS

United Nations. (2018). *Urban Population (% of Total Population) - Thailand.* Retrieved from: https://data.worldbank.org/indicator/SP.URB.TOTL.IN.ZS?locations=TH

United Nations. (2019a). *World Population Prospects 2019.* Retrieved from: https://population.un.org/wpp/Download/Files/1_Indicators%20(Standard)/EXCEL_FILES/1_Population/WPP2019_POP_F15_1_ANNUAL_POPULATION_BY_AGE_BOTH_SEXES.xlsx

United Nations. (2019b). *World Population Prospects 2019.* Retrieved from: https://population.un.org/wpp/Download/Files/1_Indicators%20(Standard)/EXCEL_FILES/1_Population/WPP2019_POP_F13_D_OLD_AGE_DEPENDENCY_RATIO_2564.xlsx

Wongsin, U., Sakunphanit, T., Labbenchakul, S., & Pongpattrachai, D. (2014). Estimate unit cost per day of long term care for dependent elderly. *Journal of Health Systems Research, 8*(4), 344–354.

Wongtanasarasin, W., Srisawang, T., Yothiya, W., & Phinyo, P. (2021). Impact of national lockdown towards emergency department visits and admission rates during the COVID-19 pandemic in Thailand: A hospital-based study. *Emergency Medicine Australasia, 33*(2), 316–323.

World Health Organization. (2020a). *COVID-19 Health System Response Monitor, Thailand.* World Health Organization Regional Office for South-East Asia, New Delhi.

World Health Organization. (2020b). *The impact of the COVID-19 pandemic on noncommunicable disease resources and services: results of a rapid assessment.* Geneva: World Health Organization. Retrieved from https://apps.who.int/iris/handle/10665/334136.

Zwi, A. B. (2021). Development trends and assistance for health. *Global Health: Ethical Challenges*, pp. 217.

5 Long-term care development in Vietnam

Thanh-Long Giang, Dai-Thu Bui, and Thai-Quang Trinh

Background

Vietnam is about to experience one of the most rapid paces of population ageing ever seen globally (Vietnam National Committee on Ageing (VNCA) & United Nations Population Fund (UNFPA) 2019). While around 8% of the Vietnamese population (around 6.5 million people) were 65 years or older in 2019, the General Statistics Office of Vietnam (GSO) (2020) estimates that this age group will reach 14.2% in 2036, meaning that Vietnam will enter a phase of a rapidly ageing population within 17 years. This demographic transition is happening in an economy which relies on family transfers and private savings as the basic sources of old-age support rather than on public social security programs. Also, rapid urbanisation and migration are eroding these sources. At the same time, the emerging middle class and their rising incomes create new possibilities and new expectations in terms of greater access to public social services (Ministry of Planning and Investment, Vietnam (MPI) and World Bank 2015). This presents both challenges and opportunities for an ageing population.

One challenge is that Vietnam has been seeking to rapidly expand social programs, including coverage of pension and health insurance, and to build an aged care system from a very low base in terms of financial, technical, and human resources (Dam 2010; VNCA and Deutsche Gesellschaft für Internationale Zusammenarbeit - German Agency for International Development (GIZ) 2012; Giang et al. 2019). One opportunity that Vietnam has is that it can adopt policies without facing an overhang of unsustainable commitments as it has been reasonably careful to guarantee only a modest basic package of benefits. An important consideration for any future government support for older persons is thus the complementarity and potential substitution of family support. Policy responses to ageing will need to cover

DOI: 10.4324/9781003131373–5

a number of areas as ageing is a multi-dimensional challenge and its impact spreads from a macro-level to individuals and households.

This chapter aims to review the existing legal and institutional frameworks and the implementation of an aged care system in Vietnam. Based on the review, advantages and disadvantages of the system are identified, and recommendations for strengthening the existing centre-supported aged care services in Vietnam are discussed. This chapter covers the following topics:

- Description and analyses of demographic trends toward an ageing and aged population in Vietnam;
- Overview and analyses of the institutional framework, service provision, financing issues, and human resources of the aged care system in Vietnam; and
- Recommendations in terms of priority developments in key areas.

In order to pursue the above-mentioned research scope, the authors used existing data and studies to provide statistical indicators such as ageing population, older persons and their care needs, and aged care provision, as well as relevant policy issues.

The chapter is organised as follows. In Section "Demographic ageing and long-term care needs in Vietnam", we provide an analysis of the demographic ageing in Vietnam and then care needs of older persons based on their performances in activities of daily living (ADLs). Section "Long-term care system in Vietnam: issues and recommendations" discusses the long-term care (LTC) system in Vietnam by reviewing its current status and various challenges in terms of institutional arrangements, services, human resources, and financing. Discussion and policy recommendations are provided in Section "Discussion and policy recommendations". The final section concludes the chapter.

Demographic ageing and long-term care needs in Vietnam

Demographic ageing in Vietnam – the past and the future

Vietnam is a country among those with the highest rates of ageing. The total population on 1 April 2009 was 85.85 million, while on 1 April 2019, it was 96.21 million (Figure 5.1), of which the older population (those aged 60 and over) was 7.45 million in 2009 and 11.41 million in 2019 (respectively 8.68% and 11.86% of the total population). On average, in the period 2009–2019, the annual growth rate of the total population was 1.14%, while it was 4.35% for the older population.

Unit: 1,000 persons

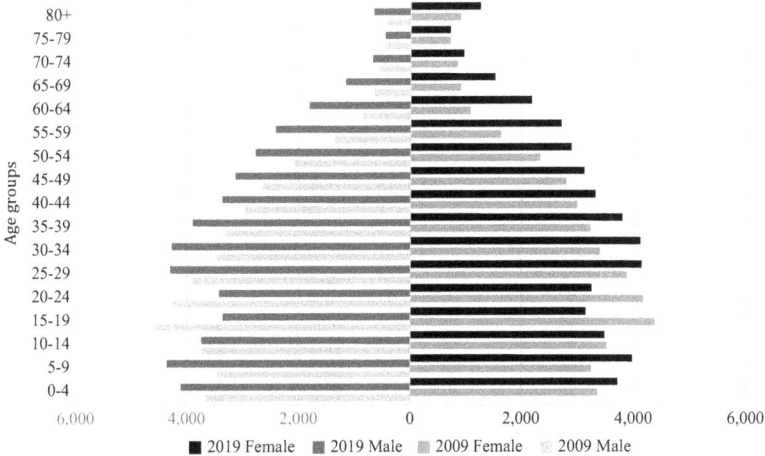

Figure 5.1 Vietnam population pyramids in 2009 and 2019
Source: GSO (2021), using data from the Population and Housing Census (PHC) 2009 and 2019.

Figure 5.2 demonstrates the distribution of the older population in 2009 and 2019 by age group and residential area (urban versus rural). Due to urbanisation, the proportion of older persons living in rural areas decreased from 72.47% in 2009 to 67.16% in 2019 (or the proportion of older persons living in urban areas increased from 27.53% to 32.84%). In both censuses, for older men and women, the proportion living in urban areas was higher for those at younger ages. In other words, the proportion living in rural areas was higher for those at more advanced ages. This is an important trend in terms of the distribution of the older population, which needs to be considered in formulating and implementing policies and services for older persons, particularly for the oldest old who tend to have high needs of care, as presented in the following section.

Changes in the population's age structure raise concerns about the sex ratio in the older population, as this indicator is a critical factor in issues such as living arrangements and widowhood, as will be presented below. Figure 5.3 shows that the sex ratio (measured by the number of older women to every 100 older men) tended to decrease over time in all age groups. At higher age groups, however, the sex ratio was higher, meaning that there were more older women than

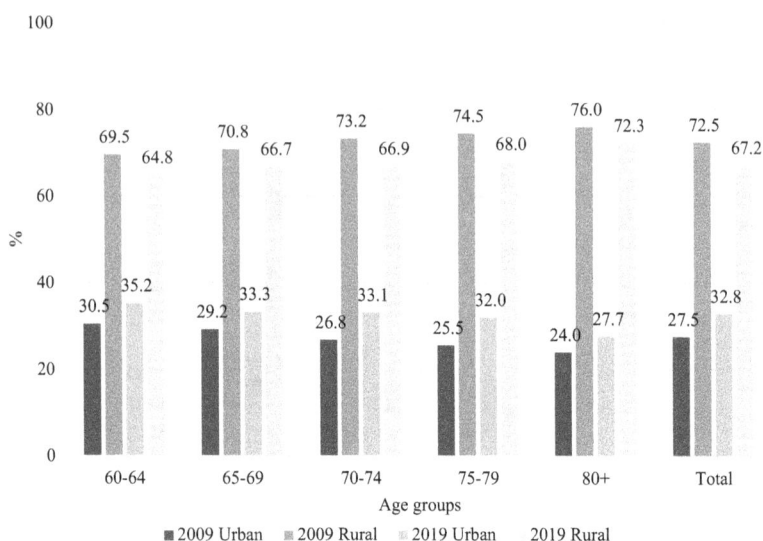

Figure 5.2 Distribution of the older population by sex and residential area, 2009 and 2019
Source: GSO (2021), using data from PHCs 2009 and 2019.

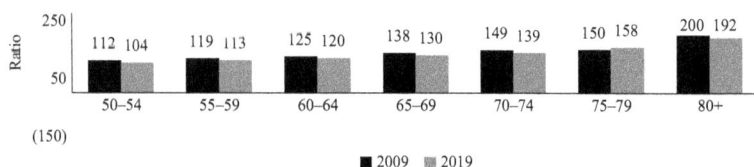

Figure 5.3 Sex ratio by age groups among the older population, 2009 and 2019
Source: GSO (2021), using data from PHCs 2009 and 2019.

older men at more advanced ages. One of the reasons for this trend might be due to differences in mortality rates between older men and older women, especially at more advanced ages (UNFPA 2011; Vietnam Women's Union (VWU) 2012). As a result of improved knowledge and awareness of health and a more accessible healthcare system, such differences narrowed between 2009 and 2019; for instance, the ratio decreased from 200 older women for every 100 older men to 192 older women for every 100 older men in the oldest-old age group. There have been some possible explanations for this situation, including that men usually have a much higher rate of health-risk behaviours (such as smoking and alcohol consumption) than women, which result in differences in mortality rates at higher ages. As will be shown later in this chapter, the feminisation of ageing among the oldest old implies a number of issues in designing and implementing aged care services.

The living arrangements of older persons in 2019 are presented in Figure 5.4. More than 60% of older persons still lived with at least one child. Among the oldest old, this rate was about 73%. Urban older persons had a much higher percentage of living with children than their rural counterparts (78.4% versus 59.8%), and this could be explained by the fact that owning or renting a house in urban areas is increasingly expensive. Older women, rural persons, and the oldest old had higher proportions of living alone than older men, urban persons, and younger persons. Rural persons had a higher proportion of living in "skip-generation households" (i.e. those with older persons living only with their grandchildren) than their urban counterparts. This might be due to the outmigration of the middle generations in these

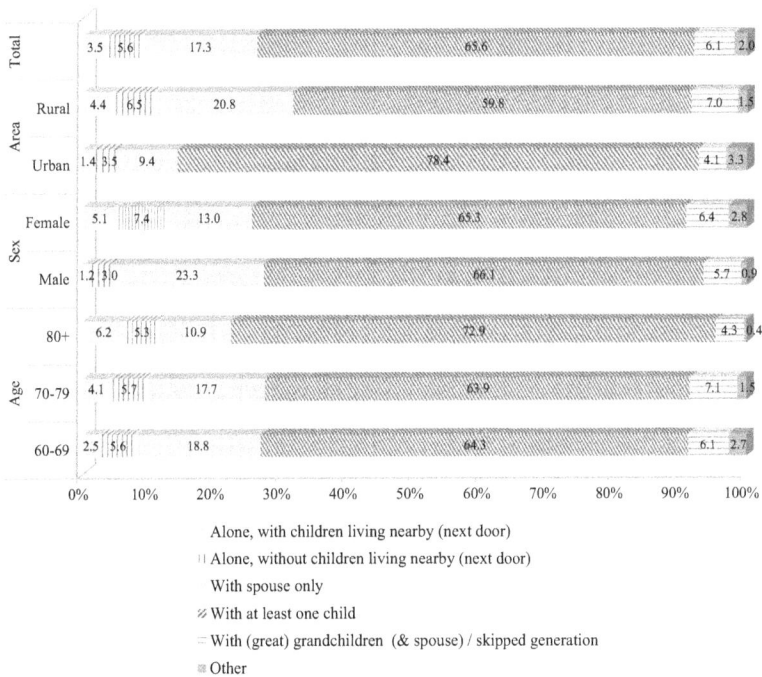

Figure 5.4 Living arrangements of older persons, 2019
Source: MOH et al. (2021), using data from Survey on Older Persons and Social Health Insurance 2019.

households. The proportion of older persons living with a spouse only was different in terms of age group, gender, and residential area. More specifically, the oldest old had the lowest rate of living with a spouse, which is due to the fact that they had a very high rate of widowhood, especially among older women. The rate of rural older persons living with a spouse only was twice the rate of their urban counterparts (20.8% versus 9.4%).

Population projections under the assumption of medium fertility rates for the period 2009–2069 (GSO 2020) show that the older population will reach 17.28 million (16.53% of the total population) in 2029; 22.29 million (20.21% of the total population) in 2038; 28.61 million (24.88% of the total population) in 2049 and 31.69 million (27.11% of the total population) in 2069. If older persons are defined as those aged 65 and over, it is projected that the Vietnamese older population aged 65 and above will reach 12.03 million (11.51% of the total population) in 2029; 15.46 million (14.17% of the total population) in 2036; 21.09 million (18.34% of the total population) in 2049; and 25.16 million (21.52% of the total population) in 2069 (Figure 5.5).

In terms of age groups, the population projections (under the assumption of medium fertility rates) in Figure 5.6 show that older persons at younger ages (aged 60–74) will increase and then decrease. In contrast, older populations aged 75–79 and 80 and over will increase continuously. In particular, the oldest-old group will have the highest growth rate and increase level: increasing from 2.1 million in 2029 to 8.75 million in 2069. Such growth implies a swift increase in care needs of older persons in the coming decades.

Based on these population projections, feminisation of ageing will occur, but it will be of less concern than indicated by figures in 2009 and 2019 as presented above. Over time, the sex ratio will decrease, particularly for the oldest old. Such projected sex ratios could be

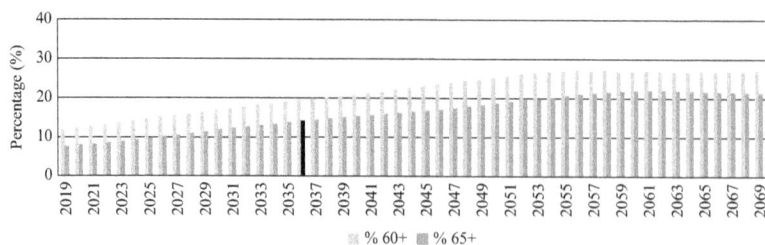

Figure 5.5 Projected percentages for older population aged 60+ and 65+, 2029–2069
Source: GSO (2021), using data from PHCs 2009 and 2019.

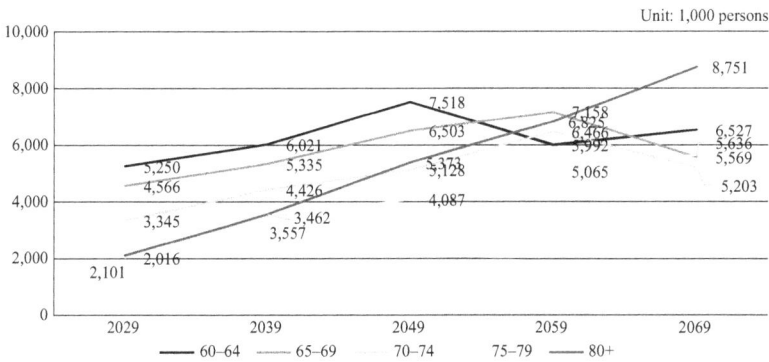

Unit: 1,000 persons

2029	2039	2049	2059	2069

Values shown on chart:
10,000 — 8,751
8,000 — 7,518
6,503 — 7,158 / 6,825 / 6,466 / 5,992
6,021 — 6,527 / 5,636 / 5,569
5,250 / 4,566 — 5,335 — 5,373 / 5,128 — 5,065 — 5,203
3,345 — 3,462 / 3,557 — 4,087 — 4,426
2,101 — 2,016

—— 60–64 ⋯⋯ 65–69   70–74   75–79 —— 80+

Figure 5.6 Projections for older population in Vietnam by age group, 2029–2069
Source: GSO (2020), using data from Population Projections for the period 2019–2069.

elucidated by the projection assumptions that the sex ratio at birth (which is measured by the number of newborn boys per every 100 newborn girls) will decrease, while the differences in mortality rates between older men and women will narrow. A noteworthy point is that in the future, as was found in 2009 and 2019, the proportion of older people living in rural areas will increase at more advanced ages (meaning that the respective proportion of older people living in urban areas will decrease). Moreover, the sex ratio in terms of age group and residential area implies that, at more advanced ages, the rate of female older persons living in rural areas will be higher than their male counterparts. Such trends once again affirm that there should be priorities in the planning and provision of services, such as LTC for older persons living in rural areas, particularly for the oldest old and older women (Le & Giang 2016; Giang et al. 2019).

Long-term care needs of older people

The LTC needs of older people include medical and non-medical care for people with chronic diseases or disabilities which make them unable to take care of themselves for a long period of time (Ministry of Health (MOH) Vietnam & Health Partnership Group (HPG) 2018). The LTC needs of older persons include assistance with ADLs such as eating, washing and bathing, and getting to and using the toilet. Figure 5.7 shows clear differences by age groups and gender for older persons in performing ADLs, in which more advanced aged persons and older

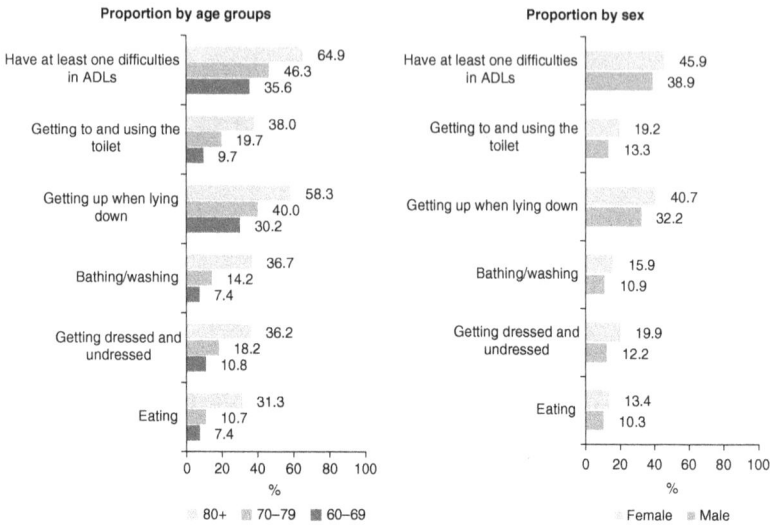

Proportion by age groups

Have at least one difficulties in ADLs: 64.9 / 46.3 / 35.6

Getting to and using the toilet: 38.0 / 19.7 / 9.7

Getting up when lying down: 58.3 / 40.0 / 30.2

Bathing/washing: 36.7 / 14.2 / 7.4

Getting dressed and undressed: 36.2 / 18.2 / 10.8

Eating: 31.3 / 10.7 / 7.4

80+ 70–79 60–69

Proportion by sex

Have at least one difficulties in ADLs: 45.9 / 38.9

Getting to and using the toilet: 19.2 / 13.3

Getting up when lying down: 40.7 / 32.2

Bathing/washing: 15.9 / 10.9

Getting dressed and undressed: 19.9 / 12.2

Eating: 13.4 / 10.3

Female Male

Figure 5.7 Percentage of older persons having difficulties with ADLs in the past 30 days, 2019

Source: MOH et al. (2021), using data from Survey on Older Persons and Social Health Insurance 2019.

women had higher proportions of difficulties than younger persons and older men. About 65% of the oldest old had at least one difficulty, while that was only about 36% for those aged 60–69, and 46% for those aged 70–79. About 46% of older women had at least one difficulty, while it was about 39% for older men. Such differences imply that care needs are heterogeneous among older persons, and as such, care services should be individual based in terms of both design and provision of services.

In terms of self-care, Figure 5.8 presents differences in age group (more advanced-aged persons had higher rates of difficulty), in gender (women had higher rates of difficulty than men), in ethnicity (ethnic minority persons had higher rates of difficulty than Kinh persons), and in residential area (those living in rural areas had higher rates of difficulty than their urban counterparts).

LTC needs of older persons are increasing partly due to an increase in the older population and increased life expectancy at birth, and partly due to social changes and limited home-based LTC (Phi & Ngo 2019). This is because family members of working age have to work and therefore cannot stay at home to care for the older persons. In

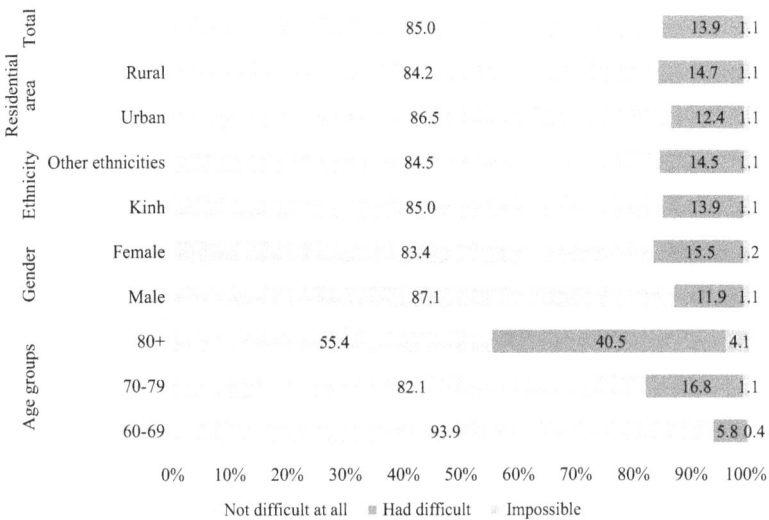

Residential area	Total	85.0	13.9	1.1
	Rural	84.2	14.7	1.1
	Urban	86.5	12.4	1.1
Ethnicity	Other ethnicities	84.5	14.5	1.1
	Kinh	85.0	13.9	1.1
Gender	Female	83.4	15.5	1.2
	Male	87.1	11.9	1.1
Age groups	80+	55.4	40.5	4.1
	70-79	82.1	16.8	1.1
	60-69	93.9	5.8	0.4

0%   10%   20%   30%   40%   50%   60%   70%   80%   90%   100%

Not difficult at all   ■ Had difficult   ▨ Impossible

Figure 5.8 Proportion of older persons having difficulty in self-care, 2019
Source: GSO (2021), using data from PHC 2019.

combining data on disability prevalence by age group in the 2009 PHC and population projection statistics for 2049, MOH & HPG (2018) projected that by 2019 approximately 1 million older people would need LTC because they would have difficulties with or be unable to perform at least one ADL. By 2049, if there is no change in the disability prevalence by age group, this figure will increase to 2.5 million (Figure 5.9). However, LTC needs may be even greater if the needs of a third of older persons who have difficulties but are still able to perform these functions are considered. Most recently, GSO, UNFPA, and Japan Fund for Poverty Reduction (2021), using data from the Population Change and Family Planning Survey 2021, showed that 6.32% of the older population (or about 796,000 older persons) found it very difficult to perform or could not perform at least one ADL, and these older persons needed substantial help or assistance with ADLs. Among these persons, there were significant differences by age (older persons of higher ages, particularly the oldest old, had a higher rate of difficulty), sex (older women had a higher rate of difficulty than older men), ethnicity (persons of other ethnicities had a higher rate of difficulty than Kinh persons), and place of residence (rural residents had a higher rate of difficulty than urban residents).

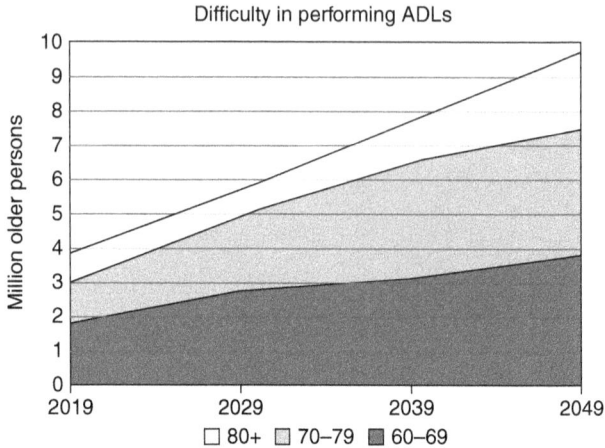

Figure 5.9 Projections of older people facing difficulties with ADLs, 2019–2049

Source: MOH and HPG (2018).

Long-term care system in Vietnam: issues and recommendations

In all the Constitutions of Vietnam since 1945, older persons have been entitled to family care and families have been responsible for taking care of older parents and grandparents. The 2009 Law on the Elderly (National Assembly of Vietnam 2009) further stipulates the rights and duties of older persons, in which children and grandchildren have the primary care responsibility. Depending on the situation, the persons in charge of taking care of the older persons should, for example, provide lodging, financial assistance, and cover healthcare costs. If the family cannot take care of the older persons, individuals and/or organisations can provide home-based or facility-based care for older persons. For disadvantaged older groups (such as older persons living alone without support or older persons living in poverty), they are provided care at social protection facilities. Those voluntarily providing primary care for older persons in the community is provided with a monthly allowance for their care work. A similar policy was also applied to the older ethnic minority people in the National Action Program for the Elderly during the period 2012–2020. The Ministry of Health (MOH) approved Decision 7618/QD-BYT in 2016 for the Healthcare for the Older Persons covering the period 2017–2025 with the target that, by 2025, all older persons who cannot perform self-care will be provided healthcare by their families and/or communities.

Institutional arrangements

This section outlines the aged care responsibilities of the main agencies and organisations. These are also presented in Figure 5.10.

The Ministry of Labour, Invalids and Social Affairs (MOLISA) is primarily responsible for matters relating to older persons. The Social Protection Department is a unit belonging to MOLISA that has the responsibility for assisting the Minister in implementing the state management of matters related to the elderly. The Ministry also has the responsibility for making and implementing policies for older persons, including LTC, regulation of professional standards for and training of caregivers, and the planning and development of social protection facilities across the whole country. According to the Decree 21/2021/ND-CP dated 15 March 2021 on social assistance policies for social protection beneficiaries, MOLISA is responsible for monitoring social protection regulations, including support for the care of older persons in the communities, social protection facilities, and social shelters. In addition to building competency standards for staff members working in social protection facilities, MOLISA is responsible for supporting activities by the Association of Social Protection Establishment Directors, examining, inspecting, and resolving complaints related to the operation of social protection establishments and submitting reports to the central government. According to the project on consolidating and expanding the network of social assistance facilities for the period 2016–2025 (Decision No. 524/QD-TTg dated 20 April 2015), MOLISA has been assigned to finalise regulations and standards for social assistance facilities.

The Provincial Departments of Labour, Invalids and Social Affairs (DOLISA) have responsibilities related to LTC for local older persons, including guiding and implementing the National Action Program for the Elderly and other relevant social protection projects/programs, aggregating data and quantifying the number of older persons to be provided with social assistance, and organising the development of the network of social protection establishments (Joint Circular No. 37/2015/TTLT-BLDT-BXH-BNV dated 29 October 2015). Evaluating applications and granting of licenses for establishing non-public care settings are the responsibility of the DOLISAs or the District Labor, Invalids and Social Affairs Divisions, depending on the type of establishment (Decree No. 06/2011/ND-CP dated 14 January 2011). At the district level, the District Labor, Invalids and Social Affairs Divisions guide and examine the implementation of social protection-related regulations. The chairpersons of the local People's Committees (provincial and district levels) are responsible for making decisions about the establishment of non-public social protection establishments operating at a province and public district level

(Decrees 68/2008/ND-CP dated 30 May 2008, and 81/2012/ND-CP dated 8 October 2012). The Business Registration Division under the Provincial Department of Planning and Investment grants business licenses to enterprises engaged in the care of older persons (e.g. nursing homes or enterprises providing home-based caregivers) (Enterprise Law and Decree No.78/2015/ND-CP dated 14 September 2015). However, before being allowed to operate, the establishment must have additional licenses depending on the field of business registration.

The Vietnam Association of the Elderly (VAE) is a social organisation representing the aspirations, rights, and legal interests of the older people in Vietnam. It is a volunteer organisation run under the Constitution, the Law, and VAE regulations. With a wide network in all provinces, districts, and communes/wards throughout the country, VAE has actively participated in various activities such as the development of policies and assistance regimes, the implementation of social security policies, and the establishment and development of different forms of clubs.

Vietnam's National Committee on Ageing (VNCA) was established in accordance with Decision No. 141/2004 QD-TTg dated 5 August 2004. VNCA is a multi-sectoral organisation with the function of assisting the Prime Minister in directing and coordinating ministries, sectors, mass organisations, and localities in dealing with issues relating to older people. In each province and district, there is a local working group on older persons' affairs responsible for studying situations of older persons, proposing solutions, and directing related organisations in their provision of aged care.

The Ministry of Health (MOH) has a crucial role in delivering health care to older people. It is responsible for guiding and organising healthcare provision at health facilities and in the community, and guiding the management of chronic diseases. Further, under the Law on the Elderly and the National Action Program for the Elderly, MOH's responsibility is to promote and implement programs on the prevention, examination and treatment of cardiovascular disease, diabetes, Alzheimer's disease, other chronic diseases, and reproductive health-related diseases. Additionally, MOH manages the implementation of programs on the prevention of disabilities and provides guidance on community-based rehabilitation for people with disabilities, including the elderly. Under MOH, various institutions, such as the General Office of Population and Family Planning (GOPFP), the Department of Health (DOH), and the District Health Center (DHC), manage different providers and services.

Other ministries with responsibilities related to aged care include:

•   **The Ministry of Planning and Investment (MPI)**: responsible for approving plans and projects related to aged care

- **The Ministry of Finance (MOF)**: responsible for allocating funding for aged care to related ministries and the VNCA
- **The Ministry of Home Affairs (MOHA)**: responsible for developing policies on organisations and salary regulation of workforces involved in aged care
- **The Ministry of Information and Communication (MOIC)**: responsible for giving direction to related organisations on information, education, and communication (IEC) for older people
- **The Ministry of Culture, Sports and Tourism (MOCST)**: responsible for supporting older people in culture, sports and tourism activities.

Provision of long-term care services

Vietnam has developed two LTC models for older persons (Figure 5.11). The dominant one is the family-based care model with additional support from the community and paid services. The other is the centralised LTC model, which is provided by public or private facilities.

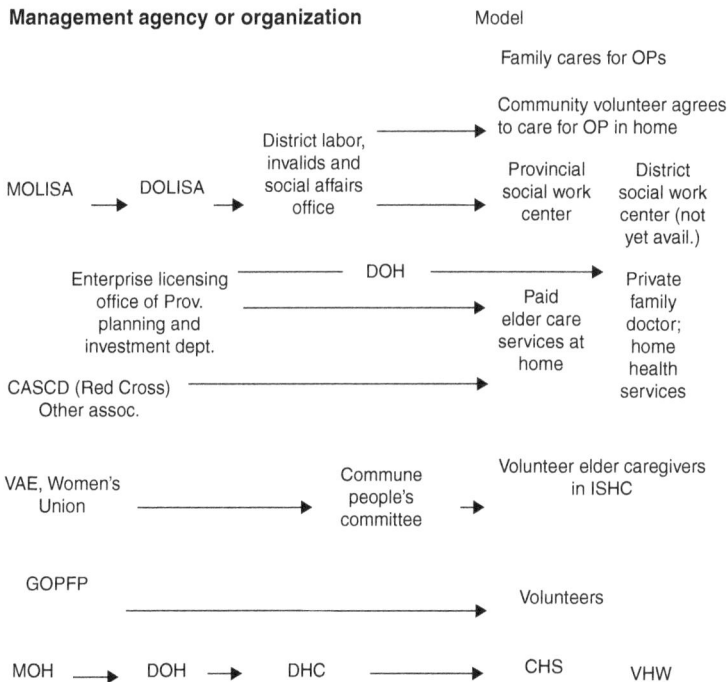

Figure 5.10 Governance of long-term care models for older persons
Source: MOH and HPG (2018).

Long-term care in the community					Institutional LTC	
	ISHCs				Public social protection center	Charity social protection center
Lower cost, subsidized	Volunteer caregivers	Social work service center, social workers	Advice and support for elder care model	CHS		
				VHW		
High cost	Paid caregivers in the home		Private family doctor, home health care services		Private eldercare facility (enterprise)	

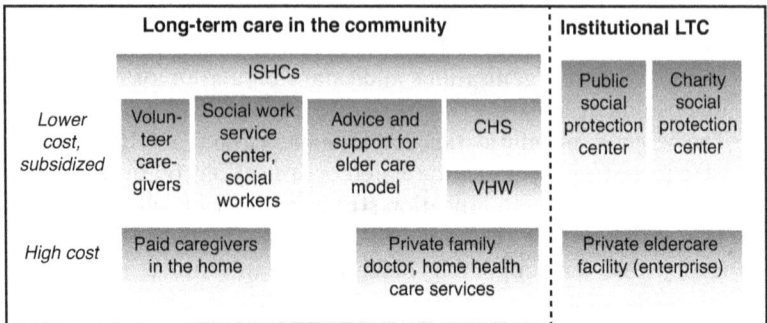

Figure 5.11 Long-term care models for older persons and their respective providers

Note: ISHCs – Intergenerational Self-Help Clubs; CHS – Commune Health Station; VHW – Village Health Worker; LTC – Long-Term Care

Source: MOH and HPG (2018).

Home-based care

Home-based care can be broad or narrow depending on the needs of older persons. Activities can include assisting with medications, arranging appropriate placement in bed, recording vital signs, and supporting in daily activities (such as bathing, dressing, and housework). Families have the legal obligation to care for their older family members; however, in some cases the care needs exceed the family's ability. Social workers only have the function of assessing needs and developing assistance plans for older persons who are social protection beneficiaries, not for other subjects such as non-poor older persons without family members obligated to care for them, or poor older persons with non-poor family members, who are nevertheless facing economic difficulties. In such cases, communities can voluntarily provide support (e.g. helping with cooking, and buying groceries).

> …My mother has been sick for a long time. I am providing care for her such as cooking, washing and feeding…
>
> (an in-depth interview with a home care-giver,
> extracted from Giang & Bui 2021)

Older persons with disabilities or severe diseases often require daily medical care in addition to assistance with ADLs. At present, the scope of home-based healthcare services is very narrow. Service providers are only allowed to implement the physician's recommendations and cannot provide prescribed medication. If an older person needs a medical examination/treatment, blood sample collection, changing of wound dressings, or medication, they have to consult with a family doctor clinic. Currently, many localities in Vietnam have no family doctor clinics. There are no regulations allowing the provision of home-based family doctor services without the physical existence of a family doctor clinic. There is also a lack of legal documents for an institutional day care model for older persons. Many older persons are still able to take care of themselves and only need support in certain areas or are suffering from mild dementia and thus should not be left home alone (e.g. people with Alzheimer's disease). However, the community-based institutional day care model has not been developed to support families to accomplish their caregiving obligations while still engaging in economic activities to generate income for the family.

> Indeed, we take care of our grandparents and parents with our love and familial duties, but we do not know the basic skills. Out-of-pocket payments are high for us if we hire personal caregivers and doctors to take care of them at home.
>
> (a FGD with district local authorities in Dong Thap province, extracted from Phi & Ngo 2019)

As contracts or commitments on aged care provisions are not standardised, it is difficult to protect older people's interests. Legal documents do provide for contracts, but do not specify the care services to be provided by primary community caregiving volunteers, volunteers, or paid home-based caregivers.

The legal obligations of family members to care for their older family members have not considered practical difficulties faced by middle-income and low-income families, or families having members employed during fixed administrative working hours. Failure to perform the obligations to care for older persons is considered an administrative violation and is subject to penalties. However, this violation is generally due to the lack of financial resources limited available time due to work commitments, or the needs of older persons with very severe disabilities exceeding family members' ability to respond. Support for families is currently only available in localities where volunteers are involved in aged care.

> In case we have to stay at home or hospitals to take care of our aged parents, we would be alternatives so that each person could be away from work for some days. Taking care of them at home is sometimes difficult, as they usually have serious sickness which requires intensive care with skilled persons. We could not do such things at home.
>
> (an IDI with a provincial authority, extracted from Phi & Ngo 2019)

Community-based care

Some socio-political organisations are involved in developing and implementing LTC models for older persons. The Red Cross Society has been active in developing care models for older persons, including the paid home-based care model. They have also together with other associations, such as the Vietnam Association of the Elderly (VAE), established care, and support centres for older persons.

The emerging community-based care model that has seen the greatest growth in Vietnam is the Inter-generational Self-Help Club (ISHC). These were piloted in 2005 and then expanded nationwide by the Prime Minister under the Decision 1336/QĐ-TTg dated 31 August 2020. These clubs are established in villages under the management of the Commune People's Committees, often headed by VAE or VWU. They aim to improve the wellbeing of older persons (particularly the disadvantaged groups) and their communities. ISHCs are self-managed, sustainable, and comprehensive. Starting with only 60 pilot clubs in Thai Nguyen province in early 2006, there are now approximately 3,500 ISHCs nationwide (VAE 2021). ISHCs have three outstanding characteristics that help promote older people's rights effectively: multiple activity areas, community ownership, and strong collaboration with local governments. A standard ISHC has at least eight activity areas, namely: (i) life-long learning, (ii) rights and entitlements, (iii) livelihood, (iv) social care, (v) health care, (vi) volunteer-based home care, (vii) self-help and community support, and (viii) resource mobilisation (HelpAge International Vietnam – HAV 2021). These activity areas encompass the rights of older people to have income security, health care, and social care. It is more convenient for older people to claim their lawful benefits through one single channel. Moreover, all activity areas are linked with each other and contribute in different ways to create a comprehensive and holistic impact (Figure 5.12).

According to Circular No. 96/2018/TT-BTC dated 18 October 2018 by the Ministry of Finance on primary health care, longevity celebration, credit incentives, commendations, and rewards, the local health commune centres must send doctors to households with older people who are sick and living alone. Nevertheless, while the demand is very high, the number of available doctors is limited (in remote areas, the ratio is one doctor per 10,000 people), and there are also limitations in local budgets and resources. ISHCs support community-based health monitoring and healthcare services. The clubs provide home-care volunteers to help a minimum of three

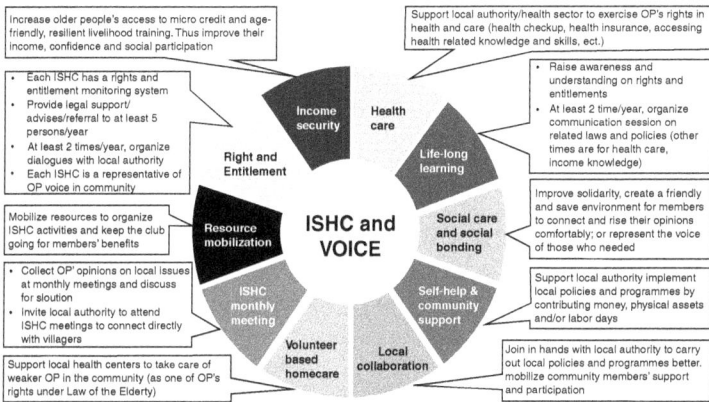

Increase older people's access to micro credit and age-friendly, resilient livelihood training. Thus improve their income, confidence and social participation

Support local authority/health sector to exercise OP's rights in health and care (health checkup, health insurance, accessing health related knowledge and skills, ect.)

- Each ISHC has a rights and entitlement monitoring system
- Provide legal support/ advises/referral to at least 5 persons/year
- At least 2 times/year, organize dialogues with local authority
- Each ISHC is a representative of OP voice in community

- Raise awareness and understanding on rights and entitlements
- At least 2 time/year, organize communication session on related laws and policies (other times are for health care, income knowledge)

Mobilize resources to organize ISHC activities and keep the club going for members' benefits

Improve solidarity, create a friendly and save environment for members to connect and rise their opinions comfortably; or represent the voice of those who needed

- Collect OP' opinions on local issues at monthly meetings and discuss for sloution
- Invite local authority to attend ISHC meetings to connect directly with villagers

Support local authority implement local policies and programmes by contributing money, physical assets and/or labor days

Support local health centers to take care of weaker OP in the community (as one of OP's rights under Law of the Elderty)

Join in hands with local authority to carry out local policies and programmes better. mobilize community members' support and participation

Income security, Health care, Life-long learning, Social care and social bonding, Self-help & community support, Local collaboration, Volunteer based homecare, ISHC monthly meeting, Resource mobilization, Right and Entitlement

ISHC and VOICE

Figure 5.12 ISHC activities for older people
Source: HAV (2021).

times per week. The volunteers remind the older person to take their prescribed medication and/or provide basic personal care. If the older person's condition worsens, local health workers will be notified. In this way, ISHCs help to reduce the workload of health workers. If volunteers receive training from authorised organisations and ISHC are connected closely with the local health sector, the quality of care will be improved. From another perspective, to help implement the MOH's Healthcare Plan for Older Persons for 2017–2025 (under Decision 7618/QD-BYT by MOH dated 30 December 2016), ISHCs host daily physical exercise sessions, monthly blood pressure and weight checks, and quarterly self-care communication. ISHCs also coordinate with the health sector to organise a minimum of two health check-ups for older persons per annum. Since all the above services are provided at the village level, they are highly accessible for older people and assist the health sector to manage community health more efficiently (Giang et al. 2020; HAV 2021).

Institutional (residential) care

Currently, the concept of "residential long-term healthcare facilities" for older persons is unclear. This is because social protection establishments currently do not provide medical services, while hospitals do not have a LTC function. In relation to LTC, the Healthcare Plan for Older Persons for 2017–2025 does not mention the role of the labour, invalids and social affairs sector and social protection centres, although Circular 04/2011/TT-BLDTBXH dated 25 February 2011 has assigned these facilities responsibility for medical care.

Residential care settings are a growing proportion of aged care in Vietnam. They provide long-term residential care, including personal and medical care, as well as "hotel services" (such as cooking, laundry, and cleaning). There are both public and non-public residential care centres under different names (such as social protection centres, charity homes, nursing homes/centres, lodges, and homes for the aged). The residential LTC model for older persons is also promoted, but in the direction of mobilising social investment capital. The Law on the Elderly encourages organisations and individuals to invest in building care facilities for older persons with preferential policies in accordance with legal regulations on encouragement of social mobilisation of activities in the fields of education, vocational training, health, culture, exercise, and environment. Based on the project on strengthening and developing the network of social assistance facilities for 2016–2025 (Decision No. 524/QD-TTg dated 20 April 2015) and the planning of the network of social assistance facilities for 2016–2025 (Decision No. 1520/ QD-LDTBXH dated 20 October 2015), by 2025, there will be 64 social protection establishments taking care of older persons nationwide.

MOLISA (2019, as cited by World Bank and Japan International Cooperation Agency (JICA) 2021) showed that, in total, Vietnam currently has 418 social protection establishments, including 165 public and 223 non-public (private-charity and private-business) social assistance facilities. These establishments are serving 42,000 social protection beneficiaries, of which 10,000 are older persons. Among these, about 2,000 persons receive care at the residential public social protection centres.

In recent years, private social protection or care centres have also emerged as a complementary model to the public social protection centres, especially in urban areas. Although there are regulations allowing private social protection centres to register as social enterprises and to receive preferential treatment in terms of land allocation, taxes, and loans, they have not yet been widely applied. Many owners of social protection centres are not aware that they can register as social enterprises.

> We now still pay 10% VAT as a normal enterprise, not like a social enterprise. Investments for our businesses are high while rate of return is not the same as possible one for, say, a trading enterprise,

and as such we need to have special policy treatment, for instance, as for a social enterprise.

(an FGD with a private elderly care center, extracted from Phi & Ngo 2019)

The standards of care at social protection centres currently focus mainly on infrastructure not on care, safety, respect, and effectively meeting the needs of older persons. There are no regulations of health-care packages for older persons at social protection centres, where many of the residents have severe functional impairments and high needs of medical care.

Organisations operating in the field of aged care must meet the same conditions as social protection establishments (Decree 06/2011/ND-CP). Labour outsourcing businesses (e.g. organisations providing home-based caregivers) must provide a deposit to cover risks and any compensations that may be required during its service provision (Decree 52/2014/ND-CP). An organisation providing home-based medical services to older persons must have a license granted by the health sector to operate as a family doctor clinic and the head of the clinic must have a family doctor degree. An organisation providing residential (inpatient) services for older persons, including medical examination and treatment, in principle, must have a license granted by the health sector to operate as a health facility. However, according to the Law on Medical Examination and Treatment, inpatient services can only be provided by hospitals. The granting of a license to a non-hospital facility for the provision of residential services to older persons is not possible. In the field of LTC, in addition to granting operating licenses, MOH is assigned to guide the prevention of disease, provision of health care, medical examination and treatment, and rehabilitation for people living in social protection establishments (Decision 524/QD-TTg in 2015). MOH is also responsible for providing guidance on medical care, physical therapy and rehabilitation for people with disabilities and mental health problems in social protection establishments (Decree 68/2008/ND-CP). The health sector is responsible for granting practice certificates to health workers in establishments which provide medical care for older persons.

Financing mechanisms for health and long-term care

Current situation

Currently, funding for LTC for older persons primarily comes from household budgets and personal savings by older persons. Financial support from the state budget or charities to LTC for older persons is mainly used for older persons who are poor, unable to take care of themselves, have no close family members to care for them or have very severe disabilities (mainly regulated in Decree 136/2013, which is now replaced by Decree 20/2021). Home-based care services and business-type care facilities providing residential care for older persons are growing in numbers but their services are very expensive compared to the financial capacity of many families. Currently, there is no LTC insurance in Vietnam. Sickness benefits from Vietnam Social Security Agency (VSS) are not applicable for workers who need to take leave to care for their older family members.

Financing older persons and their caregivers: When older persons are unable to take care of themselves and need support to perform ADLs for a long period of time, their families encounter great difficulties because they not only lack knowledge and care skills but are also under financial burden. Very few families are wealthy enough to hire home-based caregivers for older persons or place their older family members in non-public social protection centres. In many cases, family members must take leave from work, affecting the family's income. Family members who care for older persons in the community are not entitled to any social assistance payments. However, monthly social assistance payments are available to older persons or their caregivers (such as older persons living alone without support from family members). Funding for social assistance payments comes from the social security budget estimates within the decentralised local budget (Circular 29/2014/TTLT-BLDTBXH-BTC dated 24 October 2014).

The amount of social assistance payments for older persons without a retirement pension is currently very low and the number of beneficiaries is limited, as indicated in the newly issued Decree 20/2021 dated 15 March 2021, which has been in effect since 1 July 2021. People aged 80 and older who do not come from poor households, have neither close family members to care for them nor retirement pension/other monthly social assistance (e.g. people with disabilities) are provided with a monthly social assistance payment of VND 360,000 (about $US 17) (coefficient of 1 x social assistance norm). Older persons who come from poor households and have no family members to care for them are provided with a social assistance payment of VND 540,000 (or $US 26) per month (coefficient of 1.5) if they are in the 60–79 age group, and VND 720,000 (or $US 34) per month (coefficient of 2) if they are in the 80 and over group.

Since social protection centres cannot accommodate all older persons with care needs, the state has an incentive policy for voluntary primary caregivers for older persons in the community. According to this policy, older persons who come from poor households, who have no close family members to care of them, or who are unable to live in the community, are eligible for admission to social protection centres or receive care at the residence of volunteer primary caregivers in the community. Such older persons enjoy a monthly social assistance payment of VND 1,080,000 (or $US 51) (coefficient of 3). In addition, volunteer primary caregivers of elderly social protection beneficiaries in the community (i.e. these households/individuals do not have legal obligations under the Law on Marriage and Family to care for those older persons) are provided with a monthly payment of VND 540,000 (or $US 26) (coefficient of 1.5).

Older persons with severe and very severe disabilities who need support for ADLs receive special assistance entitlements. Older persons with very severe disabilities receive a monthly social assistance payment of VND 900,000 (or $US 43) (coefficient of 2.5), while older persons with severe disabilities receive a monthly social assistance payment of VND 720,000 (or $US 34) (coefficient of 2). If an older person is eligible for multiple social assistance benefits, they will receive the highest entitlement level. Family members obligated to care for older persons with very severe disabilities are provided with a monthly support payment of VND 360,000 (or $US 17) (coefficient of 1) for their care. Voluntary primary caregivers for older persons with very severe disabilities are provided with a monthly support payment of VND 540,000 (or $US 26).

Financing at public social protection centres: Older persons living in public social protection centres are covered by the state budget. The Prime Minister's Decision 1508/QD-TTg dated 27 July 2016, was that the state budget would cover social services relating to LTC for social protection beneficiaries. For older persons who are poor, have no close family members to care for them and are unable to live in the community, the government will cover the screening and admission costs; assess their needs for mid-term or LTC; provide health check-ups and primary healthcare; develop care plans; organise the implementation of care plans; provide shelters, food, clothes and other necessities for living; manage beneficiaries; provide rehabilitation; organise cultural, recreational and entertainment activities; and deliver healthcare. The state budget covers the costs of care and nourishment for older persons admitted to social protection centres. For older persons living in social protection centres or social shelters, as indicated in Decree 20/2021, the government pays the centre/shelter a monthly amount of VND 1,440,000 (coefficient of 4) per beneficiary who is poor, has no close family members to care for him/her and is unable to live in the community, or has very severe disabilities.

The cost norm for care at public social protection centres is lower than an older person's basic needs. Public social protection centres receive funding from the local budget (social security budget) to cover recurrent expenditures such as wages, electricity, and water (in line with Decision 1508/QD-TTg in 2016).

Financing at private aged care centres: Non-public (private) aged care centres receive funding from the state budget, charitable contributions or through fees paid by the older persons' families. For older persons who are eligible for admission to social protection establishments, if they are cared for in non-public establishments (charity or enterprises), these non-public/private centres will enjoy the same assistance payments for their care as public centres. Other operational expenditures may be covered by contributions from charities or the older persons' families. However, the fees at private aged care centres are often very high, generally ranging from 6 million to 13 million VND/month for basic services (such as a furnished bedroom, a shared living room, laundry, food, daily acupressure massage, personal hygiene, daily health monitoring, and physical activity). Additional services are available at additional costs.

Financing social work services: Social work services provided to older persons who are social protection beneficiaries are covered by the state budget. These services can be divided into three categories: (i) social work services (such as counselling, communication, advice, community-based rehabilitation, and prevention of harassment and violence); (ii) services related to volunteer-based care for older persons (such as care-needs assessment and development of care profiles); and (iii) home-based or centre-based residential care (such as healthcare; physical rehabilitation; and training in daily life skills). Older persons who are not social protection beneficiaries will not receive any payment for services. A key issue for this group of elderly is that there are no regulations on the price schedule of social work services.

Financing of volunteer caregivers: There have so far been no legal regulations on the financing of volunteer care work. In fact, volunteers even lose their possible income as they spend time caring for older persons instead of generating income from work. When the workload is heavy (such as caring for older persons with dementia or who are bedridden), volunteer caregivers are forced to sacrifice their income. Due to these issues, it is almost impossible to provide volunteer care at a large scale and in the long term.

Challenges in financing long-term care

The current regulation (i.e., Decree 20/2011) specifying older persons entitled to social protection is not based on actual needs. The social assistance amount is very low compared to adequate care standards. Moreover, some vulnerable groups (such as older persons with severe disabilities) are in great needs of care, but they do not have the financial ability to hire caregivers if they live alone without any family member's support. In case older persons have severe disabilities (e.g. bedridden) or suffer from diseases that require continuous care (e.g. Alzheimer's disease), care needs are likely to exceed the family's ability to meet them. The fulfilment of a family's care-taking obligations through hiring a caregiver or leaving work to stay at home and care for an older family member can cause a financial burden to the family and in some cases lead to poverty. There are no insurance policies applicable to any LTC whether it be at home or at social protection centres. In addition, social health insurance does not cover services needed by older persons such as medical care and rehabilitation at home or in nursing homes because there are no mechanisms to control the abuse of these services.

> …We have asked the People's Committee for funding for 10 years… but they said they do not have sufficient budget to support…
> (An IDI with a representative of private aged care center, extracted from Giang & Bui 2021)

Sickness benefits do not apply to sick leave in cases where workers have to care for sick older persons. This is because there are insufficient funds in the social insurance budget, and there have been great concerns about controlling abuse of social insurance funds. Remuneration for caregivers with elementary qualifications (such as volunteers or village health workers) is not adequate enough for caregivers who provide full-time day-to-day care for older persons with severe disabilities or who are in need of medical assistance in managing their chronic diseases in the community.

> …Please do not create inequality in terms of salary and salary promotion for staff working for state and private care centers… In a state care center, staff receive 4 million VND per month, but here [the private care center], staff only receive 1.5 million VND per month and this amount has been unchanged for 10 years already.
> (An IDI with a representative of an aged care center under provincial Red Cross, extracted from Giang & Bui 2021)

The ISHC model is working relatively well at a small scale and at a low cost, but the lack of funding to expand this model nationwide is significantly concerned. Due to difficulties in financing other sectors, especially at district level, it seems that provinces do not have comprehensive plans for aged care; rather, whether a policy is changed or not depends on the availability of funding. This is why the benefit amount has not changed, although the cost of living has increased.

Social organisations (such as pagodas) can offer opportunities to care for vulnerable older people through funding from various sources, including individuals and other organisations. However, such mobilisation of funding is "informal" and depends on the availability of resources.

Human resources for long-term care

Current situation

According to the Law on the Elderly in 2009, the MOH is responsible for the training and retraining of physicians, geriatric professionals, and rehabilitation practitioners. Along with MOLISA, MOH is also responsible for improving the capacity of social workers in counselling and care activities. Given the current delivery system, as discussed above, under family- and community-based care models, general practitioners are important since they are responsible for resolving common health problems in many different specialties. Older persons, however, are not only facing health problems, but also various socio-economic issues, and thus there has been a great need for integration among curative care, rehabilitation, clinical pharmacy, preventive counselling, health promotion, social work, and personal care services, and the need for appropriate human resources is therefore also high. Currently, the main workforce for LTC services provided for older people in Vietnam is organised as illustrated in Figure 5.13.

While health human resources at all levels deliver health care for older persons, the knowledge of family medicine, geriatrics and the special needs of older persons is not evenly distributed among provinces and levels (i.e. central level, provincial level, grassroots level, and preventive medical system) (MOH & HPG 2018).

Challenges for human resources

The primary caregivers for older persons are mostly family members, who tend to be overwhelmed, lack the knowledge and skills to

Assist older persons to implement:

IADLs and psycho-social support   **ADLs**   **Health care**

Professionals ↑

Doctor, physical therapist, occupational therapist

Social workers

Nurses (secondary and higher)

Paid caregivers of older persons with secondary or junior college qualifications

Paid caregivers of older persons with short-term training (2-12 months)

VHWs

Community volunteers

Volunteers who care for older persons in their own home

Laypeople

People with responsibility to care for older persons (children, grandchildren) - The main workforce for LTC of older persons

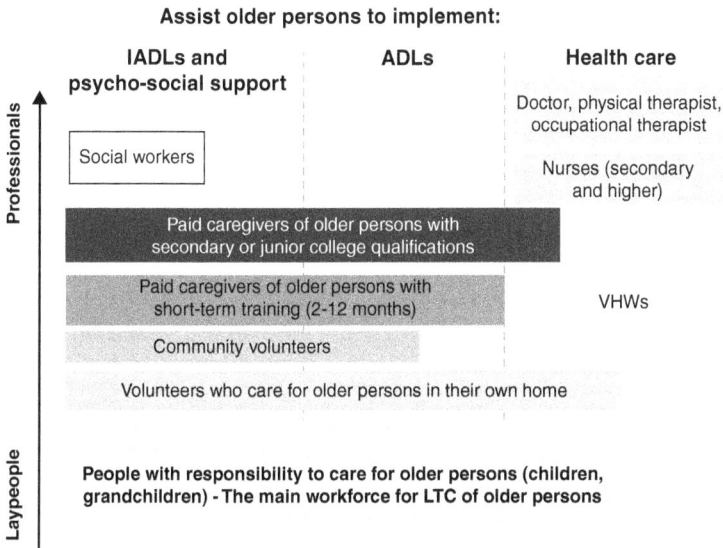

Figure 5.13 Main workforce for long-term care (LTC) service provision
Note: IADLs – Instrumental Activities of Daily Living (such as using telephone; going to market and buying neccesities); VHWs – Village Health Workers; LTC – Long-Term Care
Source: MOH and HPG (2018).

adequately care for their older family members and who do not receive any assistance or support. There is no elementary-level training available for home-based caregivers of older persons. There is a lack of quality assurance mechanisms and no electronic library which can provide video clips, lectures, and materials to guide family caregivers on how to care for older persons.

There is a lack of legal regulations on volunteer or paid caregivers of older persons. Although some community-based care models are based on volunteers or paid caregivers, there are no standardised training programs that equip such volunteers or paid caregivers with the necessary knowledge and skills to perform their tasks. The scope of work is neither specified nor is the form of service provision contract/commitment to protect the interests of older persons being cared for as well as the caregivers. There are no regulations on responsibilities nor any mechanisms for monitoring the quality of home-based care (e.g. safety, hygiene, and health management) provided for older persons.

The majority of families with aged family members are unable to hire paid caregivers. This is a key issue for families who cannot take care of their older persons at home. Generally, the cost of care, especially for those who are disabled or suffer from serious illness, is beyond the financial capacity of the older persons' families. The lack of professional caregivers at community and family levels is making care services unaffordable for many families.

> With the current costs of care for each group of older people living here, I do not think many older people and their families are able to afford the services. In particular with older people who are bedridden, the costs are varied and quite high, depending on their health status.
>
> (an IDI with a private aged care center in Hanoi, extracted from Phi & Ngo 2019)

There is a lack of staff working at public social protection centres and they are not trained in providing care to older persons. They generally lack specific care skills and do not meet the required standards. As a social protection centre has many kinds of beneficiaries, a person is in charge of taking care of various beneficiaries – from a child, or a disabled person to an older person. While different beneficiaries require different care skills, these are currently not catered for. Management in aged care is mostly based on experience rather than professional training. Competency requirements for caregivers of older persons have not been sufficiently defined to develop training materials. While caregivers of older persons are required to have experience or skills in caring for older persons (as indicated in Decree No. 06/2011/ND-CP), the lack of specific competencies makes it difficult to develop training programs for different personnel involved in the care of older persons. There is also a lack of ethical standards of personal care workers.

> Here [at the care center], we do not have any staff who have a background in social protection neither any staff who are trained in social protection.
>
> (An IDI with a representative of a private aged care center, extracted from Giang & Bui 2021)

The current pre-practice training for aged care is insufficient. Geriatric medicine is not fully integrated into the curricula of health science training programs. In such curricula, there is content related to health care for older persons, but it mainly focuses on general medical examination, treatment and care for older persons while knowledge and skills related to communication and psychology receive little attention. The medical training program (i.e. training of general practitioners) has no credit hours of training in geriatrics. The traditional medicine training program (i.e. training of traditional medicine physicians) has three credit hours on traditional medicine geriatrics. Currently, there is not a consistent geriatrics curriculum for doctors and nurses.

At present, there are geriatrics postgraduate training programs for level-I specialist doctors, level-II specialist doctors, masters, and doctorates. However, the number of training institutions is limited. Family medicine is suitable for health care for older persons, and family medicine training has been provided to physicians and specialists (level-I and level-II specialists). There is also a short-term training program for nurses, technicians, assistant doctors, and general doctors. Compared to the number of persons in need of care or assistance – both institutional and community-based care – the number of trained persons is rather small.

Discussion and policy recommendations

Vietnam has a very limited time to prepare and adapt to its rapidly ageing population. Although ageing and aged care have increasingly been part of Vietnam's strategies and policies, there is limited awareness of ageing-related matters in policy formulation and planning. More relevant laws and regulations have been issued in order to adapt or cope with an ageing population. However, policies on LTC are relatively fragmented, depending on the functions and responsibilities of the line ministries and their entities. Therefore, in order to improve the LTC system, there are a number of recommendations, as follows:

About institutional arrangements for aged care: First, the roles of VNCA, VAE, and the Social Protection Department (MOLISA) need to be strengthened in terms of developing, evaluating and revising policies related to older persons, such as health care, health insurance, social work, care for people with disabilities, social assistance, human resources, and facilities to care for older persons to make sure that special needs of older persons are considered. Second, a research program should be developed to accumulate evidence to support the development of appropriate policies on LTC for older persons. The research should focus on care needs (medical and social care), the capacity of the family and community to respond to the older person's needs, and current support from the state/local governments/charities. It should also evaluate the healthcare needs of older persons at home and at social protection centres to adjust the scope of home-based healthcare services, home-based family doctor services, and healthcare services at social protection centres (including public, charitable, and private centres). Finally, based on the results of the research on the needs and the families' response capacity, a review of the definition of social protection beneficiaries is needed in order to expand social assistance beneficiaries and care allowances to needy older persons and their families.

Aged care service provision: Under a rapidly ageing population where the family size will be smaller (due to, for example, lower fertility rate and outmigration), the capacity for families to provide care for their older family members will be limited. Alternatives to such traditional provision of aged care should therefore be made available. At the same time, institutional care provisions are diverse between the public and private sectors. Public services are provided at a low cost and are therefore affordable to the majority of older people; however, the quality of care service is low. The quality of services provided by private aged care centres, however, is relatively good and demand-based but is unaffordable to many older persons. As such, community-based care for older people should be developed since such a model will help increase access and affordability of the elderly in need.

Financing aged care services: No sustainable and feasible financial solution has been found to ensure routine health check-ups for the entire older population. Health insurance is not a suitable solution because the Health Insurance Law does not require screening services and routine health check-ups in the service package to be covered by health insurance. In addition, health insurance does not cover hearing aids and prescription glasses, so the poor have great difficulty in accessing such services to increase their ability to perform ADLs. As such, it is necessary to (i) find a financial solution from social health insurance, the state budget or other sources in order to allocate funding for routine health check-ups; and (ii) consider a financing mechanism for services to treat some disabilities such as eye surgery, provision of prescription glasses or hearing aids for poor older persons to increase access to these services.

Commune health centres (CHCs) have very limited budgets, low salaries and salary supplements which do not encourage them to manage the health of older persons effectively and actively. As such, it is necessary to reconsider their incentives and accountability in the delivery of health care to older persons at the community level in order to motivate community health workers and village health workers to be more active in managing and caring for the health of older persons.

Individual incentives for those who take care of older people should also be in place, so as to compensate for the costs of care as well as reduce the economic opportunity costs for caregivers.

Regarding human resources for aged care: There should be sufficient legal documents stipulating required competencies for health workers working with older persons (including general practitioner doctors, family doctors, and doctors in specialist departments). A competency list should be in place to ensure consistent provision of pre-service training and post-graduate programs in aged care. In particular, the current training curricula for general practitioners, family doctors, and nurses must be fully integrated and consistent so as to provide adequate medical care for older people. It is also necessary to strengthen the capacity of the National Geriatric Hospital, central and provincial hospitals, medical universities and other relevant agencies to deliver continuous training to health workers in health care for older persons, and prevention and treatment of non-communicable diseases (NCDs).

The development of updated treatment guidelines, technical training, and policy formulations should be provided by MOH to facilitate the exchange of experience among professionals in charge of healthcare for older people. At the same time, there should also be an incentive system to motivate healthcare workers to spend time counselling older patients on disease prevention, medical interventions, risk factors, and side effects during treatment.

There should be regulations on community-based rehabilitation guidelines, capacity, and skills, as these are important to help older people independently perform ADLs. Continuous training in geriatrics for health workers involved in medical care for older persons should continue to be provided with an emphasis on health counselling for older persons so that they can take care of themselves and improve their health. Health workers should also receive training in providing advice on end-of-life palliative care.

A contingent of professionals involved in healthcare for older persons need to be developed, including doctors, nurses, rehabilitation technicians, social workers, and caregivers (personal hygiene, dressing, feeding, etc.) in hospitals. Regulations of teamwork need to be formulated and linked throughout departments with elderly patients in the entire hospital.

Conclusion

The above analyses have shown that ageing population in Vietnam will be occurring swiftly in its middle-income status. The aged care system, however, has not been designed and implemented appropriately in order to respond to increasing care needs of tens of millions of older persons in the coming decades. Without timely and appropriate awareness of such a rapidly ageing population, there will be huge difficulties in adapting the existing policies or introducing new adaptive policy proposals. Along with an expected ageing population, Vietnam is experiencing the "demographic window of opportunity", and thus grasping this opportunity will promote economic growth and development, which, in turn, will help to accumulate resources for its ageing population.

With several changes in size and living arrangements of elderly households and a premature development of professional institutional care along with emerging community-based care models (such as ISHC) suggest the need for an integrated care system of families, communities, and institutions in Vietnam. Local socio-political associations (such as VAE and VWU) should further enhance their roles in implementing aged care policies since they work closely with local older persons. Older persons should be provided with monetary resources and mental health support from household members, relatives, and neighbours, and they should be encouraged to self-care as much as possible.

References

Dam, H.D. (ed.). 2010. *Elderly Care in the Socialism-Oriented Market Economy and Integration (in Vietnamese).* Hanoi: The Publishing of Social Labour.

Giang, T.L & Bui, D.T. 2021. *Developing a Diversified and Resilient Aged Care Service Delivery System in Viet Nam: Case Studies of Quang Nam and Can Tho (Unpublished monograph).* Hanoi: World Bank.

Giang, T.L., Chu, V.N & Tran, B.T. 2020. The roles of local governments in protecting rights of older people: The case of intergenerational self-help clubs in Vietnam. *Local Administration Journal,* 13 (3): 1–19.

Giang, T.L., Duong, D.V & Kim, Y.J. 2019. Factors associated with perceived health status of the Vietnamese older people. *Journal of Population Ageing,* 12 (2019): 95–108.

GSO (General Statistics Office of Vietnam). 2020. *Population Projections for Vietnam in 2019–2069.* Hanoi: GSO.

GSO. 2021. *The Population and Housing Census 2019: Population Ageing and Older Persons in Viet Nam.* Hanoi: GSO.

GSO, UNFPA and Japan Fund for Poverty Reduction. 2021. *Older Persons in Vietnam: An Analysis of the Population Change and Family Planning Survey 2021.* Hanoi: The Youth Publishing House.

HelpAge International Vietnam (HAV). 2021. Intergenerational Self-Help Club – Innovative and cost-effective community-based approach to promote healthy and active ageing in Viet Nam. Presentation at International Workshop on Active Ageing, Innovation and Application of Digital Technology in Care for Older persons in ASEAN on 10 November 2021.

Le, D.D. & Giang, T.L. 2016. Gender differences in prevalence and associated factors of multi-morbidity among older persons in Vietnam. *International Journal on Ageing in Developing Countries*, 1 (2): 113–132.

MOH (Ministry of Health, Vietnam) & HPG (Health Partnership Group) (2018). *Joint Annual Health Report (JAHR) 2016: Towards a Healthy Ageing in Viet Nam*. Hanoi: Medical Publishing House.

MPI (Ministry of Planning and Investment, Vietnam) & World Bank. 2015. *Viet Nam 2035: Toward Prosperity, Creativity, Equity, and Democracy*. Hanoi: MPI & World Bank.

National Assembly of Viet Nam. 2009. The Law on the Elderly (the Law No. 39/2009/QH12 dated 23 November 2009).

Phi, M.P. & Ngo, V.N. 2019. *Assessing Current Situation and Directions for Elderly Care System Development (unpublished monograph)*. Hanoi: World Bank.

UNFPA (United Nations Population Fund). 2011. *Aging population in Vietnam: Current Status, Prognosis, and Policy Responses*. Hanoi: UNFPA.

VAE (Vietnam Association of the Elderly). 2021. ISHC have brought real benefits for older persons and communities (in Vietnamese). Access (20 November 2021). http://hoinguoicaotuoi.vn/c/clb-lien-the-he-tu-giup-nhau-mang-lai-loi-ich-thiet-thuc-cho-nct-va-cong-dong-5548.htm

VNCA (Vietnam National Committee on Ageing) and GIZ (German International Cooperation). 2012. *Review on 2 Years of Implementation of the Law on the Elderly*. Hanoi: VNCA & GIZ.

VNCA & UNFPA. 2019. *Towards a Comprehensive National Policy for an Ageing in Viet Nam*. Hanoi: VNCA & UNFPA.

VWU (Vietnam Women's Union). 2012. *Viet Nam Aging Survey (VNAS): Key Findings*. Hanoi: Women's Publishing House.

World Bank & JICA (Japan International Cooperation Agency). 2021. *Viet Nam: Adapting to an Ageing Society*. Hanoi: World Bank & JICA.

6   Promoting long-term care in Indonesia

Maliki, Dinar Kharisma, Rosinta H.P. Purba, and Nurlina Supartini

Introduction

Indonesia is moving closer to an aging population. Currently, people aged 60 and above account for 9.9% of the total population, or about 26.8 million people (Badan Pusat Statistik [BPS], 2020). The population projection predicts that this percentage will continue to increase and reach around 20% in 2045. The government and private sector have to be ready for this change in population structure and prepare the necessary policy, programs, systems, and facilities.

So far, the availability of programs for the elderly in Indonesia is still limited. While several institutions offer long-term care (LTC) programs, these are limited in coverage, quality, and integration. Based on the pilot of the Elderly Information System (*Sistem Informasi Lanjut Usia*–SILANI) conducted in 2019 by the Ministry of National Development Planning (Bappenas) in three provinces in Indonesia, 9.7% of the elderly in the pilot regions needed LTC. These elderly recorded high Activity Daily Living (ADL) and Instrumental Activity Daily Living (IADL) scores and showed a need for assistance in performing their daily activities. Furthermore, 88.2% of the elderly with LTC needs were actually supported by at least one caregiver. To be more specific, of all the elderly who needed LTC, 78.2% were taken care of by family caregivers, 9.3% were cared for by non-family caregivers (these could include professional caregivers or community members), and the remaining 11.8%, despite their need for LTC, did not have anyone to take care of them.

In 2020, the Indonesian population was around 270.3 million (BPS, 2020). If the results from the SILANI pilot apply in the national level, at least 2.5 million older Indonesians required LTC in 2020. Of this group, close to 2 million elderly had their family members as caregivers, about 241,000 were cared for by non-family members, and

DOI: 10.4324/9781003131373–6

approximately 306,000 the elderly needed LTC, but did not have anyone to provide care for them (BPS, 2020). This situation is somewhat concerning because currently, the availability and standard of LTC programs are limited. At least three ministries, the Ministry of Health, the Ministry of Social Affairs, and The National Population and Family Planning Board, provide LTC and other care programs for the elderly in Indonesia. Additionally, LTC programs are provided by local governments and community organizations.

The Ministry of Social Affairs provides institutional care, home care, and day care for the elderly through their nursing homes and social workers (Kementerian Sosial, 2014b). They also work together with the Civil Society Organization (CSO) to expand their service coverage. The Ministry of Health provides care for the elderly through community health centers (*Puskesmas*). The Puskesmas have health workers focusing on senior care and provide curative, promotive, and preventive care (Kementerian Kesehatan, 2019b). Integrated care post for the elderly (*Posyandu Lansia*) is a promotive and preventive health activity under *Puskesmas* targeted at the elderly in the *Puskesmas* service area. The National Population and Family Planning Board creates social groups consisting of the elderly and families with the elderly. They recruit and train cadres to manage the groups and provide capacity building for the elderly and their families, and work together with *Puskesmas* in running *Posyandu Lansia*. Cadres consists of community activists and volunteer, usually in the health sector. They receive some trainings and small monetary compensation just enough to cover their operational costs. In Bahasa Indonesia, they are called *kader* which is a direct translation of cadre in English. Local governments and NGOs sometimes offer additional programs to fill the gaps and complement the national agenda to provide additional care, hire more social workers and cadres, or provide additional activities for the elderly.

However, as mentioned earlier, the coverage and quality of the programs vary greatly. Some programs have a wide coverage but with limited benefits, while others have comprehensive benefits with a small coverage. This chapter aims to provide a description of the situation for the elderly in Indonesia, the current policies and programs, and the plan to develop the policy. The chapter then presents Posyandu Lansia as a case study due to the program's data availability and relevancy with LTC developments in Indonesia. The Indonesian Family Life Survey (IFLS) data, a close-to-national representative dataset, features detailed questions on Posyandu Lansia. The chapter analyzes the data to better understand the way the program operates and the characteristics of the beneficiaries.

The elderly in Indonesia: socioeconomic status and access to care

Based on the age category, the 2020 National Socio-Economic Survey (*Susenas*) data show that 64.3% (17.2 million) of the elderly are the youngest-old aged 60–69. The remainder consists of 27.2% (7.3 million) of the middle-old aged 70–79, and 8.5% (2.2 million) of the oldest old aged 80+. The percentage of female elderly for all categories was 4.7 percentage points higher than the males.

As shown in Figure 6.1, the aging rates of Indonesian regions do not occur at the same speed. Based on the rate of people aged 60 or above, compared to the population per province, there are six provinces with a higher percentage of the elderly than the national median; DI. Yogyakarta (14.71%) has the highest proportion, followed by Central Java, East Java, Bali, and West Sumatera. Papua, on the other hand, has the smallest percentage of senior citizens at 3.6%. However, similar to the general population, the most significant number of the elderly nationally is concentrated in Java, with more than 15 million elderly (Badan Pusat Statistik, 2020).

Socioeconomic status based on Susenas 2020

The socioeconomic status of elderly Indonesians varies between regions. The elderly have a higher poverty rate than the national average poverty rate. The data also indicate that older females have a higher poverty rate than their male counterparts and that the poverty rate of the elderly increases with age (BPS, 2020).

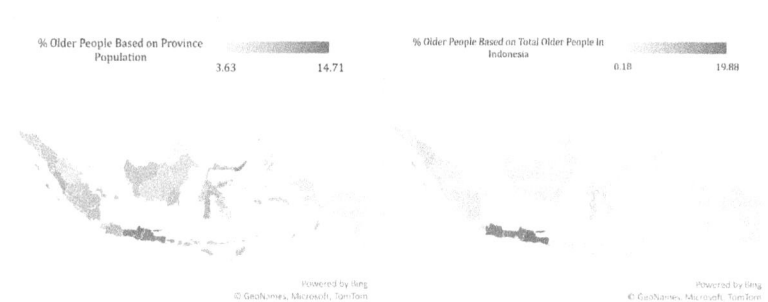

Figure 6.1 Indonesian regions based on the percentage of the elderly
Source: Badan Pusat Statistik (2020).

Nearly half of older Indonesians continue to work even though the number of working the elderly tends to decrease with increasing age. Per government regulations, the retirement ages of Indonesians range from 58 to 65 years old (Undang-Undang Republik Indonesia Nomor 13 Tahun 1998 Tentang Kesejahteraan Lanjut Usia, 1998). However, as the enforcement of these regulations is stricter in the formal employment sector, most of the elderly work in the informal sector. They predominantly work in the agriculture and forestry sectors (BPS, 2020).

The level of educational attainment of older Indonesians varies based on the age groups. Older population aged over 60 was among the first generation benefiting large number of elementary school expansions (SD INPRES). The school access was still limited to some regions, especially some remote areas. Therefore, close to two-fifths of the elderly never went to school, while 16% finished high school or above. Among the very old, more than half never went to school, and only 8.25% completed high school or university-level education. In general, older males are more likely to have attained a higher level of schooling (BPS, 2020) (Table 6.1).

Health condition

Susenas covers information on the population's health and disability status (Badan Pusat Statistik, 2020). It shows that around 13% of the elderly have a disability. Nearly half of the elderly stated that they had at least one health problem within the last month before the survey. Regarding self-care, 6.79% of the elderly face some degree of challenges to bathe, eat, dress, defecate, and urinate by themselves. The percentage of the elderly with a disability status, morbidity status, and difficulties in taking care of themselves increases with increasing age (BPS, 2020).

Finally, 65.14% of the elderly with health problems accessed health services. Interestingly, the rates are higher among the young- and middle-old than the very old (BPS, 2020). Access to health facilities and services is a challenge in Indonesia due to the geographical disparities of health facilities and availability of workers (Dorkin et al., 2014; Kharisma, 2020a, 2020b). Additionally, despite the availability, Indonesians are among the least frequent users of health care in Asia (Kharisma, 2020b). In the eastern part of the nation, such as Papua and West Papua Province, the rate of the elderly with health problems who access health care is as low as 23.10% (BPS, 2020).

Table 6.1 The characteristics of Indonesian elderly

Characteristics	Young-old (60–69) N	(%)	Middle-old (70–79) N	(%)	Very old (80+) n	(%)	Total the elderly (60+) N	(%)
Total	17,239,799	64.39	7,301,683	27.23	2,275,808	8.49	26,817,290	9.92
Gender								
Male	8,558,543	49.64	3,342,844	45.78	892,444	39.21	12,793,831	47.71
Female	8,681,256	50.36	3,958,839	54.22	1,383,364	60.79	14,023,459	52.29
Education attainment								
Never attended school/did not finish primary school	5,354,878	34.52	2,530,208	42.18	825,943	52.76	8,711,029	37.75
Graduated from primary school/equivalent	5,846,831	37.70	2,153,282	35.90	521,813	33.33	8,521,926	36.93
Junior high school/equivalent	1,561,164	10.06	497,549	8.30	88,437	5.65	2,147,150	9.31
High school or above	2,747,958	17.72	816,860	13.61	129,211	8.25	3,694,029	16.00
Job status								
Currently has a job/is in the work force	10,185,865	59.08	2,784,592	38.14	433,239	19.04	13,403,696	49.98
Formal	2,120,217	20.82	425,607	15.28	47,318	10.92	2,593,142	19.35
Informal	8,065,648	79.18	2,358,985	84.72	385,921	89.08	10,810,554	80.65
Job sector								
Agriculture and forestry	5,409,789	53.11	1,780,359	63.94	287,606	66.39	7,477,754	55.79
Trade and restaurants	2,155,534	21.16	471,877	16.95	60,367	13.93	2,687,778	20.05
Community or social services	980,549	9.63	219,870	7.90	34,398	7.94	1,234,817	9.21
Manufacturing	727,591	7.14	196,338	7.05	34,195	7.89	958,124	7.15
Other	912,402	8.96	116,148	4.17	16,673	3.85	1,045,223	7.80
Poverty rate/number of people living below national poverty line								
Male	769,772	8.99	417,387	12.49	169,414	18.98	1,356,573	10.60
Female	888,319	10.23	533,178	13.47	236,928	17.13	1,658,425	11.83
Total	1,658,091	9.62	950,565	13.02	406,342	17.85	3,014,998	11.24

House ownership								
Own house	15,968,272	92.62	6,760,113	92.58	2,094,425	92.03	24,822,810	92.56
Rent	414,327	2.40	100,120	1.37	27,706	1.22	542,153	2.02
Live in a rent-free house	821,314	4.76	429,854	5.89	151,248	6.65	1,402,416	5.23
Official residence	33,906	0.20	10,489	0.14	2,289	0.10	46,684	0.17
Other	1,980	0.01	1,107	0.02	140	0.01	3,227	0.01
Insurance and social security program								
Have at least one type of health insurance	14,027,318	81.37	6,031,910	82.61	1,806,621	79.38	21,865,849	81.54
Have National Health Insurance (JKN) coverage	11,771,239	68.28	5,023,388	68.80	1,373,415	60.35	18,168,042	67.75
Have pension or old age saving coverage	2,103,996	12.20	971,430	13.30	274,651	12.07	1,373,415	12.88
Monthly food voucher (*Sembako*)	3,029,806	11.08	1,558,848	12.39	555,215	14.25	5,143,869	11.74
Conditional cash transfer (PKH)	1,700,912	6.22	1,152,636	9.16	432,493	11.10	3,286,041	7.50
Disability status, morbidity status, and access to health care								
The elderly with disability	1,254,020	7.27	1,384,412	18.96	849,091	37.31	3,487,523	13.00
Had at least one health problem within the last month	7,958,494	46.16	3,780,630	51.78	1,171,989	51.50	12,911,113	48.14
For those with health problems, accessed health care facilities	2,525,301	65.90	1,314,221	65.61	413,925	59.56	4,253,447	65.14
Java	1,634,905	65.15	859,678	65.58	283,991	68.74	2,778,574	65.63
Outside Java	874,573	34.85	451,170	34.42	129,118	31.26	1,454,861	34.37
Independence status								
Totally dependent (*severe*)	86,902	0.50	118,525	1.62	97,129	4.27	302,556	1.13
Dependent (*moderate*)	128,743	0.75	165,628	2.27	146,382	6.43	440,753	1.64
Less independent (*light*)	326,893	1.90	454,761	6.23	297,068	13.05	1,078,722	4.02
Totally independent	16,697,261	96.85	6,562,769	89.88	1,735,229	76.25	24,995,259	93.21

Source: Badan Pusat Statistik (2020).

Current policy on elderly

Two movements are currently taking place to improve the elderly programs in Indonesia. First, a new regulatory framework was ratified through Presidential Regulation no. 88 of 2021 concerning the National Strategy for Ageing Population. This regulation includes a framework for respecting, protecting, and fulfilling the rights of the elderly in multi-sectoral areas. Second, the availability of various social security and services programs for the elderly.

Regulatory framework

The policies covering elderly in Indonesia have been based on several regulations, ranging from laws to presidential regulations. Law No. 13 Year 1998 on the Social Welfare of The elderly is the highest-level regulation governing the elderly's social services in Indonesia. However, Law No. 13/1998 sees the elderly as a vulnerable population in need of social assistance and services. This regulation has not seen the elderly as a part of the community with a potential to contribute to the economic sector. Several other regulations from the older era also have a similar tone, grouping the elderly as a generally frail community that needs help and services.

However, the new paradigm sees the elderly differently. While the current government acknowledges that some of the elderly do need social services, it also believes that most of the elderly can still be active and contribute to the economy (Burtless, 2013; Guest, 2011; Huang et al., 2019). It also asserts that the elderly have the right to be treated similarly to the rest of the population and enjoy public facilities (Baer et al., 2016; World Health Organization, 2015). One of the latest regulatory documents mentioning the elderly policy is Presidential Regulation No. 18 Year 2020 on the Medium-Term Development Planning (MDTP) of 2020–2024. As a five-year working plan of the President, produced by the Ministry of Development Planning (Bappenas), the MTDP 2020–2024 includes the elderly programs under the third national priority called "Improvement of Well-Qualified and Competitive Human Capital."

In a way, the inclusion of the elderly programs under this priority shows that the newest policy approach views the elderly as part of Indonesia's human capital. The elderly will receive capacity improvement opportunities through training and empowerment programs, including economic empowerment, elderly education, and provision of the elderly inclusive environments. In addition, this policy covers social protection programs that aim to improve quality of life. This part of the policy mandates social protection programs for the elderly, such as developing LTC programs, cash transfers, and expanding the coverage of social insurance subsidies, such as pension and health insurance.

Even though the MTDP 2020–2024 includes a more progressive view of the elderly programs and inclusion, the regulation is a general planning document with limited space for a deeper coverage of issues affecting the elderly (Peraturan Presiden Republik Indonesia, 2020). Therefore, more initiatives have been introduced to develop more specific regulation documents focusing on problems affecting the elderly. The parliament is currently in the process of revising Law No. 13/1998. However, the law is a high-level regulation and the process for change will therefore be lengthy. Therefore, the Presidential Regulation No. 88 Year 2021 on the National Strategy on Aging (NSA) was formalized recently (Direktur Penanggulangan Kemiskinan dan Kesejahteraan Sosial, 2020; Peraturan Presiden Republik Indonesia, 2021; Sinombor, 2019).

The NSA, like its name, outlines Indonesia's strategies for providing a better environment for the elderly, especially in preparation for the quickly approaching aging population (Direktur Penanggulangan Kemiskinan dan Kesejahteraan Sosial, 2020; Kementerian PPN/Bappenas, 2018). It consists of five main strategies: social protection, health status improvement, awareness of aging issues among the general community, institutions and caregivers, and rights fulfillment. Bappenas leads the development of the NSA, together with all the other ministries, including the Coordinating Ministry of Human Development and Culture, Ministry of Social Affairs, Ministry of Health, Ministry of Women's Empowerment and Child Protection, as well as the National Population and Family Planning Board. Therefore, each strategy consists of sub-strategies and ministerial-level programs to achieve the desired outcomes based on an interministerial consensus.

The NSA brings the latest vision of an aging Indonesia. Older Indonesians should be treated similarly to the rest of the population, have the same rights, and enjoy the same access to all public facilities and opportunities. Once signed by the President, ministries, and local governments are required to refer to the document when developing the elderly programs. Aged care program goals have been achieved (Kementerian PPN/Bappenas, 2018; Peraturan Presiden Republik Indonesia, 2020, 2021). Bappenas leads the monitoring process and will produce a technical regulation guiding the process.

Social protection and basic needs fulfillment

Most of the elderly are covered by at least one type of health insurance, but only a small percentage of the elderly have pension coverage or old age savings. For the elderly living in poor and vulnerable families, social assistance is available through the conditional cash transfer (*Program Keluarga Harapan* – PKH) and monthly food vouchers (*Program Sembako*).

Data from Ministry of Social Affairs (2020) show that conditional cash transfer PKH currently covers nearly 10 million poor and vulnerable families with pregnant mothers, under-five children, school-age children, persons with disabilities, and the elderly. The program provides cash transfers quarterly, requiring the families to send their children to school and utilize health care facilities. The maximum total benefit of CCT PKH is IDR10.8 million per year, or about US$750 (Kementerian Sosial, 2019; Zakiah et al., 2020). The benefit amount depends on the family structure. The older person component is IDR2.4 million (about US$167) per family per year. Currently, about 1.1 million CCT PKH families have at least one older person and therefore receive the elderly's benefit component (Zakiah et al., 2020). Through existing CCT-PKH, only elderly, who lives with eligible family, receives the benefits. While the elderly who lives alone or both members of family are elderly will not eligible for the program.

The Food Voucher *Program Sembako* provides a monthly food allowance for 18.8 million poor and vulnerable families. The program provides about IDR150,000 (about US$10) per family per month through a debit card, which the beneficiaries can use to buy groceries at designated merchants (Kementerian Sosial, 2020d). Based on Badan Pusat Statistik (2020), at least 11.7% of the elderly (nearly 5.1 million) live in a *Sembako* or rice aid beneficiary family.

In addition to the two national programs, local governments sometimes offer basic needs programs for the elderly. However, the coverage and benefits vary based on the local government's fiscal capacity and political commitment (Organization for Economic Co-operation and Development, 2019). The central and local government also provides social assistance to vulnerable groups during disaster or crisis events, including the elderly. For instance, during the COVID-19 pandemic, the central government provided additional social assistance to up to 13 million families (Kementerian Sosial, 2020e). However, there is no data available on how many the elderly or families with the elderly are covered by these programs.

The central government provides five types of social insurance programs through the National Social Security System (SJSN), including health insurance, pension, old age savings, work accident insurance, and life insurance (Asian Development Bank, 2020). The National Health Insurance Program (JKN) is highly subsidized and has near to universal coverage. More than 67.7% of the elderly have JKN coverage either through government subsidies or self-paid schemes (BPS, 2020). JKN benefit coverage is comprehensive, with very few uncovered health procedures (cosmetic and elective care) and zero co-payments. However, the other four programs, usually called employment social security, which is Pension Program, have historically only been available for formal sector workers. Not until recently, have the programs been made available to all workers. Due to the limited coverage, only 5.1% of the elderly receive pension or old age saving benefits (BPS, 2020). The remainder relies on active income from informal employment, financial support from children or other family members, and social assistance.

Social services

In addition to basic needs programs, social services are provided for the elderly (Kementerian Sosial, 2014a, 2014b). These services are conducted mainly by the Ministry of Social Affairs and non-governmental organizations (NGOs). There are several national programs under this umbrella. First, the central government, local governments, and NGOs provide institutional care through nursing homes. Nursing homes owned by central and local governments are funded publicly and comply with the minimum service standard. Private or NGO-owned nursing homes, however, vary in quality. Several NGO-owned nursing homes are government partners in providing aged care; therefore, they receive some public funding and are accredited by the Ministry of Social Affairs. Some nursing homes are not and solely rely on charity funding. The government's policy encourages aging in place- and community-based care (Kementerian Kesehatan, 2019b). As a result, very few elderly are admitted to government nursing homes, except those who no longer have access to family or community caregivers. The central government also has an institutional-based short-term training program for the elderly's economic empowerment (Kementerian Sosial, 2014a).

Second, the central government, local governments, and NGOs provide social services for the elderly in the community. These services primarily consist of home care, day care, economic empowerment, and family empowerment programs. The local governments are mandated to cover "primary level" social services, such as essential care provision, through their social workers, nursing homes, and through collaboration with NGOs (Kementerian Kordinator Bidang Pembangunan Manusia dan Kebudayaan, 2016). The central government can only provide "secondary level" social services, such as capacity development, which is also through collaboration with NGOs (Kementerian Sosial, 2020b). The most recent central government program *ATENSI* offers a specific budget for the elderly to propose necessary secondary services, such as social rehabilitation. Social workers and case managers assist the elderly in proposing suitable services.

The coverage of social services for the elderly is not universal and relatively small. This is partially due to the programs' specific target group, which mainly covers the elderly who do not have any caregivers. As found in SILANI, close to 90% of the elderly in Indonesia have caregivers, and more than 80% have family caregivers. Therefore, the elderly's need for social care programs has generally been deemed low and received little attention.

Based on 2020 data from the Ministry of Social Affairs, there are currently more than 900 nursing homes and NGOs for the elderly in Indonesia, serving nearly 200,000 the elderly both in institution- and community-based care (Kementerian Sosial, 2020a). Of these organizations, about 8% are government-owned facilities, including three large central government nursing homes focusing on economic empowerment programs for the elderly. About 6% of all care recipients (nearly 11,000 the elderly) live in the institutions. However, some are only short-term residents while attending training. The government-owned facilities, which mostly have higher capacity and funding, cover about 60% of institution-based clients. The remaining care beneficiaries receive services in the community in the form of home care and day care, predominantly provided by NGOs.

The total number of the elderly receiving social care is about 7% of Indonesia's total older population. This number seems small; however, this is similar to SILANI's finding that about 11.8% of the elderly who currently need LTC do not have any caregivers Kementerian PPN/Bappenas (2019b). Further investigation needs to be conducted to identify if all of those who currently receive government care truly need LTC. If that is not the case, which is probable since some of the social care include economic empowerment programs, then the gap between the needs and available services may be more extensive.

It is hard to analyze the financing aspect of social services provision. Currently, social services for the elderly are primarily tax-funded.

In 2020, the central government program *ATENSI* funded social services for up to 35,000 the elderly – consisting of mainly community-based care and only and a very small number in institution-based care. ATENSI's service in the community program provides a budget of about IDR 2.5 million (US$173.5) per person in a certain period, and the elderly can negotiate needed services with the case managers (Kementerian Sosial, 2020b). The local governments also provide coverage through their own budgets. However, the programs vary widely, and there is no centralized database on the type and extent of coverage of local government initiatives.

The National Population and Family Planning Board (BKKBN) conducts *Bina Keluarga Lansia* – BKL (family development program) to educate families who live with the Elderly on how to care them. *BKL* facilitates community groups consisting of the elderly's families to increase the knowledge, attitudes, behavior, and skills of elderly and elderly families to improve their quality of life. As for now, BKKBN has formed 51,074 BKL groups spread throughout Indonesia (Table 6.2).

Health programs

Health care programs for the elderly are provided through several channels, including the Ministry of Health, the National Population and Family Planning Board, the National Health Insurance Program (JKN), and local governments. The Ministry of Health conducts *Puskesmas Santun Lansia* (PSL) – *santun lansia* means polite manners toward the elderly. Puskesmas (*Pusat Kesehatan Masyarakat*) is a community health center operated by the Ministry of Health at the local community level. It provides preventive, promotive, and curative health care to all community members in the catchment area. Its services are mostly covered by JKN or are highly subsidized by the government.

Some Puskesmas also provide additional programs for the elderly based on the Ministry of Health guidelines and are called PSL. PSL services include special services for older patients by providing priority waitlists, additional discounts, and geriatric health workers. PSL also provides counseling services and home care for the elderly, even though the coverage depends on the capacity of the Puskesmas. There is no data yet on how many of the Elderly have received PSL care. However, in 2018, about 48% of 9,993 Puskesmas in the whole country had been granted PSL status (Kementerian Kesehatan, 2019a).

The JKN conducts *Prolanis* (Chronic Disease Management Program), a preventive health program to support JKN members with

Table 6.2 Summary of the elderly programs in Indonesia

Institution	Program	Coverage among the elderly	Target group
Ministry of Social Affairs	CCT PKH (cash transfer)	1.1 million the elderly (Kementerian Sosial, 2020c)	The elderly live in poor families
	Program Sembako (food subsidy)	2.4 million the elderly (Kementerian Sosial, 2020d)	Poor and vulnerable families (no specific benefits for the elderly)
	Social rehabilitation services (ATENSI and LGs programs)	About 200,000 the elderly (Kementerian Sosial, 2020a)	Poor and vulnerable the elderly in need of LTC
Ministry of Health	Puskesmas Santun Lansia	48% of 9,993 Puskesmas (Kementerian Kesehatan, 2019a)	The elderly accessing health care in Puskesmas
Ministry of Health	Posyandu Lansia	100,470 Elderly posts (Kementerian Kesehatan, 2020)	All the elderly in the catchment area
Social Insurance Administration Body	JKN	6,211,434 the elderly (BPS, 2020)	All the elderly
	Subsidized JKN	11,956,608 the elderly (BPS, 2020)	Poor and vulnerable the elderly
	Prolanis	N/A	All JKN members with chronic conditions
National Population and Family Planning Board	BKL	51,074 groups, 17–69 families with the elderly per group (Badan Kependudukan dan Keluarga Berencana Nasional, 2020)	All families with the elderly

chronic conditions, especially diabetes and hypertension (Badan Penyelenggara Jaminan Sosial Kesehatan, 2014). Not all *Prolanis* beneficiaries are the elderly, but the prevalence of diabetes and hypertension is much higher among the 60+ population. In *Prolanis*, JKN cooperates with primary care facilities, including *Puskesmas* and private clinics, to create patient groups. The groups will have planned activities, such as regular medical check-ups, health education through group meetings and home visits, and group exercise. *Prolanis* also helps the members to obtain medicines and medical consultations when needed. As mentioned above, 67.7% of the elderly in Indonesia have JKN coverage (BPS, 2020). Those with diagnosed but manageable diabetes and hypertension most likely also receive Prolanis service.

The National Population and Family Planning Board conducts a program that can be considered as both health and social services. The BKL program hires local volunteers and provides aged care training. The volunteers, who are called cadres, offer home care and day care for the elderly in their service regions. Based on the Board's 2021 data, there are 214,878 hired cadres (Badan Kependudukan dan Keluarga Berencana Nasional, 2021b); however, only about 20% have been fully trained. Because the program is volunteer based with only limited benefits, it is difficult to apply specific criteria for the cadres. Some cadres are well-trained health workers, social workers, or university-educated, while many are not.

Other than conducting home care and day care, some of the BKL cadres' services include educating the elderly's families in providing care (Badan Kependudukan dan Keluarga Berencana Nasional, 2020). They also provide basic motivational training and counseling to improve the elderly's mental health. In conducting the program, the cadres have to form groups consisting of families with the elderly in their service regions. The size of the groups varies, but as an illustration, in the Kulonprogo district, Yogyakarta, which is a typical rural region in Java, there are 35 BKL groups, each consisting of between 17 and 69 family members (Kabupaten Kulon Progo, 2021). More populated urbanized regions may have larger groups, and rural regions outside Java may have smaller groups. There is at least one cadre facilitating each group. In 2021, the Board reports that their village cadres have established a total of 51,074 BKL groups across Indonesia (Badan Kependudukan dan Keluarga Berencana Nasional, 2021a).

Historically, the National Population and Family Planning Board has cooperated closely with the Ministry of Health, which is also the case with *Puskesmas* and BKL cadres. *Puskesmas,* regardless of their PSL status, conduct *Posyandu Lansia* (Integrated Service Post for The

Elderly) together with the cadres. *Posyandu Lansia* aims to improve the elderly's health status, both physically and psychologically. *Posyandu Lansia*, conducted regularly at the village or sub-village level, is primarily community driven, involving families, community leaders, social organizations, and the elderly themselves in its operations.

Posyandu Lansia focuses on promotive and preventive health care, including referral services to curative and rehabilitative facilities. Most of the services are free, but some *Posyandu Lansia* provides fee-based additional care. Based on the *Puskesmas'* guidelines for providing aged care (2004), some services in *Posyandu Lansia* include:

- supervision of daily activities, including eating/drinking, walking, bathing, dressing, getting into and out of bed, urinating, and defecating
- mental health assessment
- nutritional health assessment
- blood pressure, hemoglobin, and blood sugar check
- referral service to *Puskemas* if there are complaints or anomalies
- counseling and health education
- home visits by cadres accompanied by health workers.

Human resources at *Posyandu Lansia* typically consist of a team of health workers (doctors, nutritionists, midwives, or community health nurses) and cadres. *Puskesmas* set *Posyandu Lansia* as one of their screening mechanisms in identifying undiagnosed health problems, hence the various health checks that are included in the program. *Posyandu Lansia* is financed through diverse sources, including the *Puskesmas* budget, community contributions, and service charges. For example, funding of some *Posyandu Lansia* in the DI Yogyakarta Province comes from community dues and service fees (Kumudaningsih, 2019). The Ministry of Health report that by 2019, there were 100,470 *Posyandu Lansia* regularly operating in Indonesia. However, the frequency and activity coverage vary depending on the available resources in the region.

The elderly access to *Posyandu Lansia* and other community activities

This section analyzes the Indonesia Family Life Survey (IFLS) 2014 (fifth wave) data. IFLS or *Sakerti* is a multi-level (individual, household, community, and facility levels), multi-topic, large-scale, longitudinal survey that has been conducted in five waves since 1993. Among others, the survey covers information on access to *Posyandu Lansia* and additional information such as the characteristics of *Posyandu Lansia* and their patients. Even though IFLS is reasonably comprehensive, the sample coverage is not as extensive and nationwide as Susenas. IFLS 2014 covers only 24 of the total of 34 Indonesian provinces. The covered provinces are the most populated ones, so the survey represents 83% of the Indonesian population (RAND Corporation, 2014). However, due to a substantial amount of missing data on the elderly, only 1,321 observations are included in this analysis after data cleaning.

Characteristics of Posyandu Lansia users

Based on IFLS data, the elderly's visit rate to *Posyandu Lansia* is 16.3%, which in turn is dominated by the young old (80.1%). As expected, no very old person attended *Posyandu Lansia*. Since *Posyandu Lansia* is a community activity requiring the participants to come to a certain center, this may not be suitable for very old people or people who have difficulties in conducting physical activities. A majority (59.9%) of *Posyandu Lansia* visitors are female. There is also a greater tendency for the elderly who live in Java and more urbanized regions to participate in *Posyandu Lansia*. This is probably due to better infrastructure and access since health care facilities and workers are greater in number in Java and urban areas.

In terms of employment status, most of the elderly who participated in *Posyandu Lansia* are those who still work (71.1%). However, very few have employment in the formal sector. Around 72.4% of the elderly participating in *Posyandu Lansia* are informal sector workers who are self-employed in either the services or agricultural sector. While this information needs further verification, it may be attributed to socio-economic status. The elderly with formal sector jobs and a higher socio-economic status may not actively participate in community activities. This may also be due to work flexibility, especially if the *Posyandu Lansia* is held during work hours.

In terms of health status, most of the elderly coming to *Posyandu Lansia* have a chronic condition (69.8%). This figure is higher than the general morbidity rate of the analyzed sample, where only 55.5% of the sample have a chronic condition. This suggests that the elderly with chronic conditions need the benefits of health checks, counseling, and other programs from the *Posyandu Lansia*.

There are two purposes for the elderly to participate in *Posyandu Lansia*. The first is to access primary health services or to obtain other benefits such as food and hobby. The second is to participate/ help as a volunteer in running *Posyandu Lansia*. For those who seek the *Posyandu Lansia* benefits, the purposes of participating include receiving health checks, obtaining food supplements, meeting with other elderly, and attending health education sessions. The elderly who help as volunteers typically participate by assisting the health workers or cadres, providing food and refreshments, or donating funds to the *Posyandu Lansia* operation. Almost all who visited

Table 6.3 Characteristics of the elderly attending *Posyandu Lansia*

Characteristics	Posyandu Lansia attendees	General the elderly
Number of the elderly		
Total sample	232	1,321
% of young-old	79.31	76.31
% of middle-old	20.69	22.48
% of very old	0.00	1.21
Gender		
% of male	40.09	57,68
% of female	59,91	42,32
Living location		
Urban	68.53	67.60
Rural	31.47	32.40
Java	78.45	57.76
Outside java	21.55	42.24
Employment status		
Working	71.12	71.84
Housekeeping	28.88	16.27
Retired	0.00	6.81
Disable/sick	0.00	3.03
Other	0.00	2.05
Chronic disease status (hypertension, diabetes, heart disease, stroke, cancer, high cholesterol, kidney disease, emotional, dementia)		
Yes	69.83	55.49
No	30.17	44.51
Purpose of visiting *Posyandu Lansia* (not mutually exclusive)		
For accessing benefits	49.13	n/a
Health check	36.86	n/a
Receive food/supplements	16.38	n/a
The elderly regular meetings	21.84	n/a
Togetherness/hobby	13.65	n/a
Education	11.26	n/a
For volunteering	93.10	n/a

Source: IFLS (2014).

Posyandu Lansia come to assist (93.1%). Only about half required some type of service. Among those who do require services, most either need a health check (36.86%) or attend the elderly meetings (21.8%) (Table 6.3).

Posyandu Lansia services and facilities

IFLS data surveyed 525 *Posyandu Lansia* across 15 provinces. Of these, 70.29% are in Java and Bali, the most developed parts of Indonesia, confirming that *Posyandu Lansia* is primarily available in the most populated and urbanized areas. Cadres and midwives have a prominent role in providing the services. Among the surveyed *Posyandu Lansia*, a range of services were provided by cadres (27.40%) and midwives (23.80%); followed by nurses and doctors (20.40% and 14.00% of *Posyandu Lansia*, respectively), and a small number was contributed by community members.

Puskemas, as one of the program owners, regularly supervises the *Posyandu Lansia*. Midwives are the main supervisors, representing 43% of *Posyandu Lansia*. Nurses manage 27%, and doctors supervise 19%; the remaining Posyandu Lansia are supervised by nutritionists and public health officials. Concerning the operational aspect, more than 80% of the *Posyandu Lansia* face obstacles related to funding, medicine supplies, inactive cadres, lack of support from *Puskemas* and villages, and non-permanent facilities. Lack of funding is the biggest obstacle in all regions, experienced by 63% of surveyed *Posyandu Lansia*. Furthermore, *Posyandu Lansia* outside Java faces relatively more complex problems than those in Java and Bali regions such as infrastructure and access.

Participation in training programs is one indicator for identifying the skills of *Posyandu Lansia's* staff member. Only 45.5% of those operating *Posyandu Lansia* have received any training. The percentage of those who have received specific training in supporting the elderly's health is even smaller. Of all *Posyandu Lansia* operational managers, 30.3% have participated in aged care training, 26.3% have participated in nutrition training, and 22.7% have received environmental and sanitation training. As mentioned earlier, not many cadres have higher education. IFLS suggests that among those running *Posyandu Lansia* activities, only 17.9% have a university-level degree. Most have only graduated from high school or junior high school (48.4% and 24.5%, respectively) (Table 6.4).

Table 6.4 Quality and capacity of *Posyandu Lansia*

Characteristics	Posyandu Lansia in Java	Posyandu Lansia outside Java	All Posyandu Lansia
Number of Posyandu Lansia	356	169	525
Members of service providers (%)			
Doctors	14.0	17.49	15.20
Midwives	23.8	27.38	25.03
Nurses	20.40	17.11	19.27
Village midwives	10.60	7.98	9.70
Cadres	27.40	27.38	27.39
Community members	3.80	2.66	3.41
Supervisor assigned by Puskesmas to lead Posyandu Lansia (%)			
Nurses	28.21	24.58	27.00
Midwives	32.00	30.93	31.65
Nutritionists	8.21	10.59	9.00
Doctors	17.89	21.61	19.13
Village midwives	12.00	11.02	11.67
Public health officers	1.68	1.27	1.55
The capacity of *Posyandu Lansia* management (%)			
Received any training	44.67	47.33	45.52
Received aged care training	30.33	30.17	30.29
Received nutrition training	23.03	33.13	26.29
Received environmental and sanitation training	20.78	26.62	22.67
Education attainment of Posyandu Lansia leaders/supervisors:			
University level	13.99	25.92	17.87
Lower than university level	86.01	74.08	82.13

Source: IFLS (2014).

Discussion: developing integrated programs of the elderly care in Indonesia

Based on the analysis, some issues need to be addressed by the new LTC scheme or other aged care programs. The issue that needs to be addressed is the current lack of availability of adequate LTC programs in Indonesia. Current programs vary significantly in terms of coverage and quality. Some programs with very comprehensive benefits, such as nursing homes, have minimal coverage. They only target the elderly with extreme needs, such as neglected the elderly who currently do not have any family or suitable living conditions. The less comprehensive the program, the more extensive the coverage is. For instance, the PSL and *Posyandu Lansia*, which provide less intensive and less regular services, arguably cover the most Elderly beneficiaries. The situation where different institutions provide services to the elderly exacerbates the issue. Coordination is necessary when a range of organizations target the same group, the elderly. Without proper coordination, the services will be fragmented and less holistic.

LTC needs to be able to satisfy the needs of the elderly regardless of where they live, i.e. whether they live in densely populated areas such as Java, or rural areas. One issue is that the lack of available nationwide data on the actual needs of aged care in Indonesia. It is therefore challenging to determine whether the available services are sufficient. As one of the largest institutional care providers, the central government can only provide short-term empowerment programs for active the elderly who do not have any health issues. This reduces the number of available spaces for more vulnerable elderly in need of nursing homes. In addition, the more comprehensive LTC programs are not always targeted to the elderly in greatest need of assistance or the ones who are neglected, widening the gap between available services and actual needs.

Another issue is the lack of well-qualified LTC programs. The central government provides the highest standard of institutional care; however, the quality is in general still low. With more restrictive funding, local governments and NGOs typically offer less adequate service quality for both institutional and community-based services. Social workers and health cadres – paid and hired by the central government and NGOs – are the main care providers for the elderly. However, they have limited skills and are generally not well-trained in both health and geriatric care. The quality and availability also vary across islands and provinces. Additionally, it is important to note that more than 80% of senior care is provided not through government or NGOs, but by family members, usually female members. Further, it increases quality concerns since most family caregivers have even less knowledge of aged care.

To develop more long-term aged care program in Indonesia, several measures are required: (1) increase the data availability of the elderly and their needs, (2) improve the comprehensiveness and availability of aged care, (3) enhance the quality of aged care and its caregivers, (4) secure sustainable funding for the programs, and (5) reduce the disparity in aged care between the elderly in different social-economic groups and regional locations.

Currently, there are no national data collection programs that collect sufficient information on the elderly's conditions and needs. The data on vulnerable people have been based primarily on socio-economic and disability conditions, but not other standardized physical and mental health measurements. Therefore, it has been difficult for governments and NGOs to adequately plan care programs and budgets for aged care. The lack of data also has arguably contributed to the lack of general awareness of the elderly's issues. While not all issues have been appropriately addressed, Bappenas has begun addressing some of the problems, Bappenas developed SILANI (*Sistem Informasi Lanjut Usia* – The elderly Information System) as the comprehensive data collection of the elderly.

SILANI collects information that other national surveys and censuses have not included (Direktorat Penanggulangan Kemiskinan dan Pemberdayaan Masyarakat Kementerian PPN/Bappenas et al., 2020a, 2020b). SILANI data collection includes questions on participants' ADL/IADL condition, geriatric depression scale, and signs of dementia. Some questions have been remodeled to maintain the questionnaire's simplicity. The SILANI instrument has also been discussed and agreed upon by line ministries and academics. In addition to health conditions, SILANI covers information on the elderly's needs (e.g. social assistance, social insurance, home care, and empowerment programs); availability and characteristics of the elderly's caregivers; and aged care service providers in the area, including social workers, cadres, *Posyandu Lansia*, *Puskesmas*, other clinics, nursing homes, and hospitals.

Equipped with a Geographic Information System (GIS) data, SILANI takes the form of a census that includes all the elderly in a particular location. SILANI allows social workers and cadres to collect data to better understand the population group they support as well as information on available resources in their surroundings. Currently, SILANI has been piloted in several villages, covering nearly 30,000 the elderly (Direktorat Penanggulangan Kemiskinan dan Pemberdayaan Masyarakat Kementerian PPN/Bappenas et al., 2020a, 2020b). The data have been used in government planning as an indication of national LTC needs. It has also informed the government of the funding needed to provide adequate programs. During the COVID-19 pandemic, SILANI has helped governments provide social protection, health needs, and vaccines to vulnerable the elderly in the pilot locations (Direktorat Penanggulangan Kemiskinan dan Pemberdayaan Masyarakat Kementerian PPN/Bappenas et al., 2020a, 2020b).

There is a need to expand SILANI, preferably nationally, as an adequate tool for the government and other organizations in developing aged care. It has to be updated regularly and integrated with mainstream data collection, such as the census or social registry, so the national social database will also have information on the elderly's vulnerabilities. Consequently, training for data collection has to be improved to include indicators describing the conditions of the elderly. Furthermore, as an information system, SILANI can also be optimized to facilitate a digital platform connecting the elderly with case managers, caregivers, service providers, or even other elderly.

Once SILANI manages to collect data covering most of the country, it should be easier to start identifying the gap between available services and the needs of aged care. The next step to optimize the quality and availability of aged care would be to integrate various services provided by multiple ministries and institutions. Social workers, cadres, and health workers need to develop a working forum to address the elderly's needs in certain regions. By pooling together all the resources and skillsets, the team should be able to plan more effectively targeted programs or interventions needed by the elderly.

Through integration, limited resources can be optimized to support the most urgent cases. Additionally, an integration of services will allow knowledge exchange, both formally and informally, among different caregivers, improving their overall capacity. The initiative to integrate various elderly services at the community level is currently being piloted, involving three ministries with the most prominent aged care programs, the Ministry of Social Affairs, Ministry of Health, and Population and Family Planning Agency (BKKBN), coordinated by Bappenas. The integration pilot is taking place at the SILANI pilot location, allowing it to reap the benefit of SILANI's comprehensive data.

The inter-sectoral coordination and integration have occurred in an informal setting at the implementation level, where various program managers from different institutions establish their coordination forum such as MoH with Integrated Service Hub for the Elderly. However, the disconnection of the program has to be addressed at multiple levels, including at the central government level. One solution would be the enforcement of Presidential Regulation No. 88 Year 2021 on the National Strategic of Aging. NSA mandates coordination between institutions in respect, protection, and fulfillment of the rights of the elderly. The aim of the mandate would be to ensure improvement in coordination of the various aged care programs across different levels.

While an integration will help improve the LTC programs' targeting and effectiveness, it will not eliminate the need for an expansion and quality improvement of the programs. All programs need to expand their coverage to include a greater number of the elderly to fulfill current needs and preferably to prepare for future needs. Early results of

SILANI, combined with other data, can be used to estimate the needs of aged care services and plan for a gradual expansion. Nevertheless, non-government services are also crucial as most of the elderly who need LTC receive care from non-government sources, such as family members, community social workers/volunteers, privately-paid professional caregivers, or NGOs. While the government's role is expected to increase, the non-government contribution will still be significant. A mechanism to encourage family, community, and private sectors' involvement in care provision is essential to ensure the needs of the elderly are met.

Since many institutions and organizations provide care, including family and community members, national guidelines or standards of basic geriatric care for the elderly and LTC programs need to be established. Aged care, such as institutional care, home care, and day care, regardless of provider, needs to meet the minimum requirements, especially in terms of quality and service coverage. *Posyandu Lansia*, for instance, has the potential to provide an effective day care program, if there is improvement in services, coverage, quality of care, and frequency of services. Training of cadres and social workers will need to be standardized to be able to conduct case management, suitable home care, and data management, especially in the community and family. The introduction of national standards for aged care will ensure that even though multiple ministries provide aged care services, they will comply with the minimum requirements.

However, because *Posyandu Lansia* offers limited services, it will not cover the LTC needs of the elderly, especially of those who face significant challenges in conducting daily activities. *Posyandu Lansia* only provides services once in a while with limited time of program coverage. The results of the IFLS analysis have shown that most of the *Posyandu Lansia* attendees were healthier and the youngest old. Indonesia will need more comprehensive, standardized, and tailored programs to provide care for the older groups of the elderly who need more intensive care. Such care can be provided either institutionally or in the community by trained health and social workers with certification in geriatric care.

National guidelines and standards should also regulate qualifications for informal caregivers as they will continue to have a significant role in providing aged care services. Family or community members providing care to the elderly should be encouraged to attend basic training in home care. Since caregivers are overwhelmingly family members, this is one of the most important strategies in ensuring all the elderly receive good quality care. The training should be widely available, easy to access, free of charge, and adapted to the participants' different backgrounds. The mainstreaming of this program should be intensified, and incentives, support, or compensation may need to be provided to boost participation.

Additionally, a strategy may need to be developed to address the disparity in availability of health and social workers as well as facilities between different regions in Indonesia. While it may be challenging to ensure immediate equality, priority could be offered to regions with a greater aging rate. These areas could receive greater support in preparing their facilities and human resources to provide better quality and more expansive care for the elderly.

To ensure full expansion and quality improvement in aged care services, adequate funding is crucial. Currently, most aged care programs are funded by tax through various ministries. Limited funding from the National Health Insurance (JKN) Program is available for primary and preventative health care and is sometimes allocated to the *Posyandu Lansia* fund. However, many urgent aged care services are not covered by any insurance, such as nursing home services, home care, or day care.

Reforms need to be encouraged to develop more sustainable financing for a more comprehensive aged care system. Subsidies and tax-funded programs may need to remain to cover services for the poor and vulnerable. However, an initiative to include aged care services in the social insurance scheme, especially those under National Social Security System (SJSN), needs to be discussed. This would allow the cost of aged care to be divided between different funding resources. The more affluent group of the population would be able to contribute to cover the cost of their aged care while the government provides resources for the poor and vulnerable. The health insurance, pension, or old age saving programs could be enhanced to include basic aged care or LTC benefits.

Finally, a greater awareness of aging-related issues is needed, including that Indonesia is moving toward an aging population. This needs to be integrated into the development of a LTC program. The attention of policy and lawmakers is crucial to gain political support for program changes and budget increases. Awareness of the general population is, however, also urgent. Public support and appreciation of aged care programs will strengthen the programs' expansion and improvement strategy. Greater knowledge of the aging process and its corresponding needs will also influence people's treatment of the elderly in their communities and preparing for their own old age, especially by participating in social insurance programs.

128   *Maliki et al.*

References

Asian Development Bank. (2020). *Reforming the Social Security System in Indonesia*, Manila. https://www.adb.org/sites/default/files/publication/28596/ino-social-security-reform.pdf

Badan Kependudukan dan Keluarga Berencana Nasional. (2020). *Panduan Bina Keluarga Lansia Integrasi*, Jakarta. https://golantang.bkkbn.go.id/publikasi_golantang/9/download

———. (2021a). *SIDUGA BKKBN.*

———. (2021b). *Sistem Informasi Keluarga (SIGA).* Unpublished data.

Badan Penyelenggara Jaminan Sosial Kesehatan. (2014). *Panduan Praktis Program Pengelolaan Penyakit Kronis (PROLANIS).* BPJS Kesehatan.

Badan Pusat Statistik. (2020). *Survei Sosial Ekonomi Nasional (Susenas)*, Jakarta.

Baer, B., Bhushan, A., Taleb, H. A., Vasquez, J., & Thomas, R. (2016). The right to health of the elderly. *Gerontologist, 56*, S206–S217. https://doi.org/10.1093/geront/gnw039

Burtless, G. (2013). The Impact of Population Aging and Delayed Retirement on Workforce Productivity. *SSRN Electronic Journal*, May. https://doi.org/10.2139/ssrn.2275023

Komazawa, O., Suriastini, N. W., Mulyanto, E. D., Wijayanti, I. Y., Maliki, & Kharisma D. D. (2020a). *Laporan Studi Survei Telepon Lanjut Usia dan Covid-19 Di Indonesia_2020.* SurveyMETER, Economic Research Institute for ASEAN and East Asia (ERIA), dan Kementerian Perencanaan Pembangunan Nasional/Badan Perencanaan Pembangunan Nasional (Bappenas).

Direktorat Penanggulangan Kemiskinan dan Pemberdayaan Masyarakat Kementerian PPN/Bappenas, UNFPA, & SurveyMeter. (2020b). *Laporan Analisis Data Pengembangan SILANI di 7 Kab-Kota_r.* UNFPA.

Direktur Penanggulangan Kemiskinan dan Kesejahteraan Sosial. (2020). *Tanggapan: White Paper "Pemenuhan Hak-Hak Lansia untuk Hidup Setara, Sejahtera, dan Bermartabat."* The Prakarsa, Jakarta.

Dorkin, D., Li, R., Marzoeki, P., Pambudi, E., Tandon, A., & Yap, W. A. (2014). Health Sector Review: Supply Side Readiness. Kementerian Perencanaan Pembangunan Nasional. Retrieved from http://aiphss.org/wp-content/uploads/2015/02/Supply-SideReadiness.pdf

Guest, R. (2011). Population Aging, Capital Intensity and Labour Productivity. *Pacific Economic Review, 16*(3), 371–388. https://doi.org/10.1111/j.1468-0106.2011.00553.x

Huang, W. H., Lin, Y. J., & Lee, H. F. (2019). Impact of Population and Workforce Aging on Economic Growth: Case Study of Taiwan. *Sustainability (Switzerland), 11*(22), 1–13. https://doi.org/10.3390/su11226301

Kabupaten Kulon Progo. (2021). *Satudata Kulon Progo.*

Kementerian Kesehatan. (2019a). *Indonesia Masuki Periode Aging Population.* https://www.kemkes.go.id/article/view/19070500004/indonesia-masuki-periode-aging-population.html

———. (2019b). Pedoman Untuk Puskesmas Dalam Pemberdayaan Lanjut Usia. In *Pedoman Untuk Puskesmas Dalam Pemberdayaan Lanjut Usia*. Kementerian Kesehatan, Jakarta

———. (2020). *Rencana Aksi Direktorat Jendral Pelayanan Kesehatan 2020–2024*. https://e-renggar.kemkes.go.id/file2018/e-performance/1-466080-3tahunan-541.pdf

Kementerian Kordinator Bidang Pembangunan Manusia dan Kebudayaan. (2016). *PMK No. 25 Tahuun 2016 Tentang RAN Kesehatan Lanjut Usia Tahun 2016–2019*.

Kementerian PPN/Bappenas. (2018). *Keputusan Menteri Perencanaan Pembangunan Nasional/Kepala Badan Perencanaan Nasional Nomor KEP. 102/M.PPN/HK/08/2018 Tentang Pembentukan Panitia Antar Kementerian/Non-Kementerian Penyusunan Rancangan Peraturan Presiden Tentang Strategi Nasional Kelanjutus* (p. 7). Kementerian PPN/Bappenas.

———. (2019). *Sistem informasi lanjut usia (SILANI)*. Ministry of National Development Planning of the Republic of Indonesia.

Kementerian Sosial. (2014a). *Modul pendampingan pelayanan sosial lanjut usia*. Kementerian Sosial, Jakarta.

———. (2014b). *Pedoman asistensi sosial lanjut usia melalui lembaga kesejahteraan sosial*. Kementerian Sosial, Jakarta.

———. (2019). *Pedoman Pelaksanaan PKH Tahun 2019* (pp. 1–69). Kementerian Sosial, Jakarta. https://pkh.kemsos.go.id/dokumen/PEDOMAN PELAKSANAAN PKH 2019.pdf

———. (2020a). *Data panti jompo dan lansia penerima manfaat di Indonesia*. Unpublished data.

———. (2020b). *Dokumen Penganggaran Program Rehabilitasi Sosial 2020*. Unpublished data.

———. (2020c). *Pedoman Pelaksanaan PKH 2020*. Kementerian Sosial, Jakarta.

———. (2020d). *Pedoman Umum Program Sembako 2020*. 9(2), 187–205. Kementerian Sosial, Jakarta

———. (2020e). *Respon Dampak COVID-19, Kemensos Berikan Bantuan Sembako untuk Lansia*. https://kemensos.go.id/respon-dampak-covid-19-kemensos-berikan-bantuan-sembako-untuk-lansia

Kharisma, D. D. (2020a). Healthcare Access Inequity within a Social Health Insurance Setting: A Risk Faced by Indonesia's Jaminan Kesehatan Nasional (JKN) Program. *Bappenas Working Papers*, *3*(1), 63–74. https://doi.org/10.47266/bwp.v3i1.56

———. (2020b). Social Health Insurance to Protect People: A Case Study of the Impact of Indonesia's National Health Insurance - Jaminan Kesehatan Nasional (JKN) Program. *ProQuest LLC*, *68*(1), 1–12.

Kumudaningsih, D. A. (2019). Pelaksanaan Posyandu Lansia Melati Dalam Meningkatkan Pelayanan Kesehatan Di Rw 01 Kelurahan Demangan Kecamatan Gondokusuman Yogyakarta. *Kemampuan Koneksi Matematis (Tinjauan Terhadap Pendekatan Pembelajaran Savi)*, *53*(9), 1689–1699.

Organization for Economic Co-operation and Development. (2019). *Social Protection System Review of Indonesia, OECD Development Pathways, OECD*, Paris (https://doi.org/10.1787/788e9d71-en). https://www.oecd.org/social/inclusivesocietiesanddevelopment/SPSR_Indonesia_ebook.pdf

Peraturan Presiden Nomor 88 Tahun 2021 tentang Strategi Nasional Kelanjutusiaan.

Peraturan Presiden Republik Indonesia. (2020). Peraturan Presiden Republik Indonesia Nomor 18 Tahun 2020 Tentang Rencana Pembangunan Jangka Menengah Nasional 2020–2024. In *Rencana Pembangunan Jangka Menengah Nasional 2020–2024* (p. 313). https://www.bappenas.go.id/files/rpjmn/Narasi RPJMN IV 2020–2024_Revisi 28 Juni 2019.pdf

RAND Corporation. (2014). *IFLS*. The Indonesia Family Life Survey (IFLS). https://www.rand.org/well-being/social-and-behavioral-policy/data/FLS/IFLS.html

Sinombor, S. H. (2019). *Strategi Nasional Kelanjutusiaan Menunggu Ditandatangani Presiden*. https://www.kompas.id/baca/utama/2019/08/21/114225664/

Undang-Undang Republik Indonesia Nomor 13 Tahun 1998 Tentang Kesejahteraan Lanjut Usia (1998).

World Health Organization. (2015). *World Report on Ageing and Health*. WHO, Luxembourg. http://apps.who.int/iris/bitstream/handle/10665/186463/9789240694811_eng.pdf;jsessionid=B2F6F187AE492A1F9FDB78D5E538071D?sequence=1

Zakiah, K., Lestari, V. P., & Putra, H. D. (2020). Akuntabilitas Pelaksanaan Program Keluarga Harapan (PKH) Komponen Kesejahteraan Sosial (Lanjut Usia Dan Disabilitas Berat) Di Indonesia. *Pusat Kajian Akuntabilitas Keuangan Negara, Badan Keahlian DPR RI*.

7 Syntheses and ways forward

*Vasoontara S. Yiengprugsawan
and John Piggott*

Key considerations for long-term care frameworks

Demographic transitions are occurring before social protection systems have achieved wide coverage and are able to provide sufficient support for the elderly. As described in Chapter 2, family sizes have declined; the number of women in the labour force is increasing, resulting in fewer women available to caring for older persons. Meanwhile, chronic non-communicable diseases and co-morbidities often increase and become more complex with age, requiring skilled care. While demand for long-term care (LTC) policies is a growing (and urgent) demand, the process, however, is gradual and public investment in LTC supply (e.g., care facility and human resource) is to date very modest. Notably, countries covered in this book have large populations and there is an anticipation of a surge in demand for LTC — within the next 15 years, care needs will in fact more than double in these countries.

LTC systems and services that are affordable, equitable, efficient/ effective, and sustainable already exist in current conceptual frameworks. These concepts incorporate not only individual older persons and their environment but also integrated social and health services that empower older persons to remain at home and within their communities. At the same time, experience from richer countries suggests that there is no standard model of LTC systems. Three concepts from the country studies are aligned with three intrinsically linked principles for the wellbeing of older persons (ADB 2022): *first,* **"healthy ageing"**, the process of developing and maintaining functional ability within an environment that enables well-being in older age and the role of health and LTC at different stages and requirements of ageing and older persons; *second,* **"ageing in place"**, emphasises individuals ageing safely in their own home or within their communities as

DOI: 10.4324/9781003131373-7

long as possible and transitioning to residential care only as required. Ageing in place also fits well within emerging economies, especially with home and community care; and *third*, "**integrated people-centred health services**" which focus on empowering older persons to actively take charge of their own health (e.g., through health promotion and primary health care) and which offer coordinated services for older persons and their caregivers.

In the context of LTC development across the four chapters, key drivers include national ageing policy directions and the main responsible agencies – nationally and locally (whether these are within health or social sectors, or complementary). LTC policy framework considerations take into account population coverage (whether universal or subject to needs and other eligibility criteria such as income), public-private funding sources and payment mechanisms, and service provision both in health and social care at different levels.

Long-term care financing schemes and sustainability

A major challenge across all the case study countries is their financing mechanisms. The three key issues are: (i) the source of funding and mobilisation of financial resources, (ii) the balance between public cost-sharing and out-of-pocket expenditure, and (iii) the respective roles of public investment from local and national governments in LTC. For example, Japan and the Republic of Korea have established LTC insurance systems that are separate from healthcare insurances and focus primarily on older persons. These have the advantage of cost-sharing amongst individuals, employers, and general tax systems with defined eligibility and benefits packages.

As outlined in Chapter 3, the Chinese regional LTC programs have been established as pilot LTC insurance schemes which are mostly financed by the current healthcare system. These programs initially covered urban areas with severely disabled elders and were later expanded to also cover semi-dependent residents in rural areas. The Chinese case study provides insights into three different financing mechanisms for pilot LTC programs, including partial funds from the medical care system (Shanghai); medical care accounts and government subsidies, including from the welfare lottery (Qingdao); and an individual contribution with the pooled medical care account fund transfer (Nantong).

While China has a reasonably developed LTC policy framework with a means-tested poverty alleviation scheme, Thailand and Indonesia have expanded their community health services as a foundation for LTC. In Thailand, the government has estimated that universal coverage for community-based LTC for only those with severe dependency would be about 0.16%–0.22% of gross domestic product (ADB 2020). Currently, government revenue is the financing source for pilot home-based LTC programs. Thailand has also provided an example of engagement from local government for LTC through the Local Health Fund (LHF), a matching fund from the Universal Coverage Scheme and local government as a strategic financing mechanism for community-based LTC. In Indonesia, limited funding from the National Health Insurance (JKN) program is available for primary and preventative health care and is sometimes allocated to fund existing elderly community organisations. However, there is a need for a financing mechanism for nursing home services, home care, or day care. LTC would require subsidies and tax-funded programs to cover services for the poor and vulnerable. According to Intergenerational Self-Help Club (ISHC), in order to scale up and ensure financial stability, it is estimated that the Vietnamese government needs to invest 0.04% of GDP over the next decade to have 100,000 ISHCs covering every village in Vietnam.

Health and long-term care service provision

A key decision concerns whether to set up a stand-alone LTC system or to cover LTC within the existing public health-care system based on historical policy arrangements in each respective country. Effective LTC services reduce risks such as inappropriate or overuse of acute healthcare services. Governments may choose to provide LTC services directly to ensure availability to those who need it. In the case of Japan and the Republic of Korea, the provision of services is covered through a network of providers including home-based, community, and institutional private services. As outlined in the China case study, Qingdao provides a complete range of LTC from residential to nursing homes, whereas Shanghai and Nantong mainly focus on home (social) care packages. In all three cases, eligibility for LTC is evolving and is being reformed due to demand and expansion.

  In addition to providing subsidies and grants for LTC service uses, governments may assist providers based on the number of beds and other professional facilities. For example, China recently allocated an estimated CNY 1 billion for the construction of nursing homes in rural areas, which will be operated by community providers. In Indonesia, community-based services integrate health and social care needs through the collaboration between government-run health clinics (*Puskesmas*) and elderly posts (*Posyandu Lansia*). Because these services are provided at the community level, they are accessible for older people and link to health services more efficiently. In Vietnam, ISHC has taken advantage of public-private partnerships, which has strengthened the capacity of its existing local clubs to partner with the health sector and provide check-ups, preventive information, and community support for older persons.

Human resources in long-term care

There are several challenges in human resource management, including a shortage of local care workers and unequal distribution of health personnel (Tsuita Y, Komazawa O. 2020). Case studies in Thailand, Vietnam, and Indonesia highlight an established network of health volunteers from which to build and sustain good support practices for family caregivers. Policy development could focus on more and better qualified human resources for formal and informal training of family members, volunteers, caregivers, and health workers. Other issues include standardised training and professional-certification programs and improved quality-management protocols for private and public sector care providers, in particular standardised training for case management and proper home care in the community. For LTC systems across these countries, government policy encourages ageing in place and community-based care, including establishing support for family caregivers by either directly financing caregivers or subsidising use of LTC facilities. An expansion in service coverage, improvement in and standardisation of care quality, frequency in activity, and an expansion of community-based LTC models in Vietnam, Indonesia, and Thailand would require deeper government support and monitoring.

Concluding notes

Overall, LTC is a *multisectoral issue* encompassing social policies for older persons and caregivers, labour market participation, and investment in age-friendly environments. LTC is not just an individual or family issue. It will need to be addressed by communities, the private sector, non-government organisations, and governments via integrated policies, programs, and partnerships.

Challenges remain in implementing the **necessary coordination** amongst governing bodies responsible for LTC, which often resides with the Ministry of Public Health, the Ministry of Social Welfare, and the Ministry of Finance. Notably, Japan and South Korea provide examples of how integrated care agencies and case managers coordinate their services, and China and Thailand have introduced similar designated roles. Through efficient integration of services, limited resources are optimised.

Additionally, whilst the Indonesian case study highlights the need for **increasing data availability of older people and their needs**, the implementation of the pilot SILANI (*Sistem Informasi Lanjut Usia* – Older People Information System) in Indonesia and longitudinal data, such as the Viet Nam Ageing Surveys (VNAS), have helped to coordinate multisectoral data on older persons. For example, SILANI Geographic Information System (GIS) data provide information about the quality and availability of services across islands and provinces, such as the availability of caregivers and service providers in the area. Strengthening the sharing of health and LTC data will be crucial in assessing the needs and planning for service provision and human resources supply.

Community-based LTC service models are prominent across country book chapters; however, **planning for services in rural and urban areas is not homogeneous** depending on the strength, availability, and distribution of existing social and healthcare services. The majority of the emerging LTC models are piloted, such as in regional China and certain areas of ISHC in Vietnam, and *Posyandu Lansia* in Indonesia. Thus, a nationwide roll-out of these LTC policies and services will need to consider demographic and socio-economic diversity across areas in terms of availability, quality, and coverage of services. While the care for older persons in urban settings is different to that of sparsely populated areas, common challenges nevertheless exist, such as LTC coverage, quality, and comprehensiveness of care. In China and Vietnam, the demand for services is being met by engaging private providers for home care and day care at community centres. Exploring **innovative public-private partnerships** will help satisfy new demands for LTC in emerging countries. These programs may provide feasible, integrated home- and community-based care models for other low- and middle-income countries. As public systems expand, the need for better regulation and quality assurance will grow and place new demands on those overseeing LTC systems.

While emphasising home- and community-based care is an efficient choice, there may be gaps in care which would require advanced medical care, particularly for those with severe care needs such as dementia and palliative care. Social aspects of LTC will not replace but will support family based informal care in the case of high needs, specialised care and respite for caregivers. In addition, support and training of caregivers is of vital importance to provide care for the older persons' families and in the broader community. Last but not least, *not only coverage of long-term care is essential but also allowing consumer choice and ensuring its quality.* Integration of formal and informal care and service expansion as well as monitoring and quality assurance will be important considerations as LTC systems develop.

References

ADB. 2020. *Country Diagnostic Study on Long-Term Care in Thailand.* Asian Development Bank, Manila.

ADB. 2022. *The Road to Better Long-Term Care in Asia and the Pacific: Building Systems of Care and Support for Older Persons.* Asian Development Bank, Manila.

Bei L. (forthcoming). China long-term care programs. In. Yiengprugsawan V.S., Piggott J. eds. *Shaping Long-Term Care in Emerging Asia: Policy and Country Experiences.* Routledge Taylor & Francis Group, London and New York.

Chuakhamfoo N.N., Yiengprugsawan V.S., Pannarunothai S. (forthcoming). Public long-term care in Thailand. In. Yiengprugsawan V.S., Piggott J. eds. *Shaping Long-Term Care in Emerging Asia: Policy and Country Experiences.* Routledge Taylor & Francis Group, London and New York.

Tsuita Y, Komazawa O. 2020. *Human Resources for the Health and Long-Term Care of Older Persons in Asia.* Economic Research Institute for ASEAN and East Asia (ERIA), Jakarta and Institute of Developing Economies, Japan External Trade Organization, (IDE–JETRO) Tokyo.

Long G.T., Bui D.T., Trinh Q.T. (forthcoming). Long-term development in Vietnam. In. Yiengprugsawan V.S., Piggott J. (eds.) *Shaping Long-Term Care in Emerging Asia: Policy and Country Experiences.* Routledge Taylor & Francis Group, London and New York.

Maliki, Supartini N., Kharisma D., Purba R. (forthcoming). Promoting long-term care in Indonesia. In. Yiengprugsawan V.S., Piggott J. (eds.) *Shaping Long-Term Care in Emerging Asia: Policy and Country Experiences.* Routledge Taylor & Francis Group, London and New York.

World Bank. 2016. *Live Long and Prosper: Aging in East Asia and Pacific.* World Bank, Washington, DC.

Index

For Product Safety Concerns and Information please contact our EU
representative GPSR@taylorandfrancis.com
Taylor & Francis Verlag GmbH, Kaufingerstraße 24, 80331 München, Germany

www.ingramcontent.com/pod-product-compliance
Lightning Source LLC
Chambersburg PA
CBHW061744270326
41928CB00011B/2363

* 9 7 8 0 3 6 7 6 7 4 5 9 5 *